HEALING
SPIRITUAL
WOUNDS

CAROL HOWARD MERRITT

HEALING SPIRITUAL WOUNDS

RECONNECTING *with a*

LOVING GOD

AFTER EXPERIENCING

a HURTFUL CHURCH

HarperOne
An Imprint of HarperCollinsPublishers

FIRST EDITION

Designed by Ralph Fowler

Library of Congress Cataloging-in-Publication Data
Names: Merritt, Carol Howard, author.
Title: Healing spiritual wounds : reconnecting with a loving God after experiencing a hurtful church / Carol Howard Merritt.
Description: New York, NY : HarperOne, [2017]
Identifiers: LCCN 2016039345 (print) | LCCN 2016048979 (ebook) | ISBN 9780062392275 (hardcover) | ISBN 9780062392282 (e-book)
Subjects: LCSH: Spiritual healing--Christianity. | Spirituality--Christianity. | Religious fanaticism--Christianity. | Religious addiction--Christianity.
Classification: LCC BT732.5 .M467 2017 (print) | LCC BT732.5 (ebook) | DDC   248.8/6--dc23
LC record available at https://lccn.loc.gov/2016039345

17 18 19 20 21   LSC   10 9 8 7 6 5 4 3 2 1

To

Beth Sentell

and

Matthew Buell

Contents

Chapter 1

A TREE GROWS IN MY BEDROOM

I paced the small room, wringing my hands as if sopped with foul dishwater. *What should I do?* I breathed the question through choppy gasps as I listened to the human explosion down the hall.

Fear choked me as I heard the voices of my mother and father, rising and cresting, with angry rhythm. I tried to figure out my strategy if it became dangerous. I could barge into the living room with some sort of demand and start redirecting my father's rage toward me. I regularly used that trick because my dad had never hit me, and so the interruption would confuse his fury. But it worked better when my sister was caught in the snare of argument. When my mom was fighting, my intrusion could just make the violence worse.

What should I do?

I thought about my bank account. I started it as soon as I could and filled it with as much exit money as I could gather. My classmates spent their money at the mall, but I'd been saving mine for a while. I had to have a plan. I had older friends who would take me in when it got too bad, but I didn't think I could leave yet. I didn't have enough money and I had too much time before college. No one had enough patience for somebody else's teenager invading her space for three years.

What should I do?

I walked from one corner to the other, from my bookshelves to my bed, a simple path, back and forth, so small that it almost made me dizzy. My mind, in contrast, felt like a complicated labyrinth as I tried to figure my way out.

What should I do?

I could run to the neighbor's house again, but my mom warned me that they would call child protective services if I kept going to them for help. Then she filled my head with enough foster care horror stories to make me fear I'd be jumping from a scary ledge into the heart of a volcano. If I left, I needed to do it on my terms. But what were my terms?

What should I do?

Our family was an upstanding Christian family. I had gone to the church for help, but their teaching— that my father was the head of the house and we needed to submit to him—seemed useless now.

What should I do?

The voices grew louder. Dishes banged and clattered. I stood next to my door and tried to figure out if it was from jerky, angry handling or throwing. I didn't think he was throwing things. Not yet.

I had no place to turn, and so I went back to my wringing, pacing, and asking, *What should I do?* until it became a chant. I added an address to my pleading, and it was a prayer. *O God, what should I do? God, what should I do?* I muttered as fear overwhelmed me.

Then, as if I entered the eye of a tropical storm, peace blew its hot, humid breath. My feet stilled, but not out of panic. I looked down at my hands and they were motionless too. I inhaled smooth, deep air. The sense of normalcy was such an odd feeling that I sat on my bed and listened to the breath coming out of my mouth in wonder. I closed my eyes and placed my palms up on my lap. I no longer heard the fighting. I wasn't sure if it actually stopped, but I didn't hear it any longer. Instead, this overwhelming sense that it would be okay—that I would be okay—flooded me. God surrounded and embraced me.

I became altered so much in that moment that I was sure I was breathing God. I didn't know exactly how, but I understood it to be as true as the oxygen that filled my lungs. I had a sudden realization that I was living, moving, and being in *God*. The solitary event altered my outlook in such a way that it marked me internally with a "before" and an "after." BCE and CE—Before the Carol Era and the Carol Era.

Something grew in the room beside my bed and bookshelves. It was a tree—a spiritual tree but still vivid to me. The gnarled twisting roots burrowed deep into the rug and the foundation, and they kept plunging, through the earth's crust and into the mantle. I could feel the branches hunched with the wearied exhaustion of carrying the weight of the world for so many years, while the hardy trunk looked as if it had stood up to the most bullying hurricanes.

If I could get a good look at its vivisection, I had no doubt that the rings would prove its ancient history. But I had no desire to cut it down. Instead, I imagined plucking a great piece of fruit from its drooping limb and biting into it. It would be bursting with intense hybrid flavors, a genetic splicing of an apple tree with horseradish. For me this connected to the Seder meal, where on the same plate we combined the bitter herbs of horseradish and the sweetness of the apple.[1]

The meal was a reminder to the people of Israel that life was full of bitterness and sweetness. Sometimes they both came on one plate. In my conjured vision of that Saturday morning, both flavors mixed in one fruit. I savored the sweetness of my life, family, and religion, but I also knew it tasted bitter at times. My years encompassed the intensity of this contrast.

As I breathed in my complicated peace, I prayed that God would protect my mother. I asked that God would give me compassion for my father. I prayed for the courage to forgive. As I chewed on that fruit, it wasn't as if the peace lulled me into complacency and made me want to stay in the house. Instead, it gave me a connection with God and strength to leave when I could.

GETTING PAST MY INNER SKEPTIC

A skeptic lives inside me. Just as my memories come with fictional fruit trees attached to them, this inner skeptic also comes out to play among my recollections. With a little jab at my rib cage, he says, "Oh, how nice. God, your imaginary friend, arrived just in time! But if God had time for house calls, don't you think that God would be with the starving kids in Haiti rather than with your little privileged white self?"

I smile at my skeptic and keep telling the story, even if it makes me ridiculous. There are some spiritual experiences that I cannot fully explain, and doing so may make me sound naive. But they are my truth, and so I take a determined step right over my cynic and his morbid chuckle. I keep moving, making a leap of faith. While in mid-jump, I grasp hold of these narratives because they contain a veracity

that a stripped-down history could not. I remind
my skeptic that we're not rewarded for suffering.
God has preference for the poor, but the Holy One
doesn't show up like a gold medal for the Oppression
Olympics. I just noticed God more in the midst of
heartache, because of my need. But God was always
there, just as God is in Haiti.

And as for God being imaginary, God's presence
in my bedroom arrived like a substance. It was like
the sweet high of the epidural hitting a spine after
hours of muscle-straining, sweaty labor. The peace
I experienced felt like prolonged sleep, an ache-less
back, or the ability to walk. It's one of those things
you don't recognize unless you've lived without it;
but if you've been in turmoil for a long time, then
peace takes on a particular palpability. It is as real as
cerulean blue.

That was how I spent my teen years, with that
complicated bittersweet relish surrounding me.
Fully knowing that religion had been complicit in
the violence, I still searched for spiritual peace. I
had many things to offer me solace, things into
which I readily submerged—friends, books, art,
and nature. They all served as retreats from the
chaos at home.

Yet they all seemed grounded in God. When
friends cared for me, I noticed something divine in
them. When I read books, a faithful wisdom emerged.

When I painted, I sensed a connection with a Spirit, a muse I channeled, or perhaps she channeled me. When I walked, a holy Otherness enlivened my senses. As I got older, I would find many more comforts in things like philosophy, wine, or sex. In all of these things, God opened doors for me, giving me access to rooms in my being I didn't know existed, and I continued to find God grounding everything that gave me life and healing.

It has been thirty years since that morning that I breathed God in the midst of my anxiety. Even after all this time, my mind regularly drifts back to that little room. It's home base in life's hectic games. It's where I'm safe. It's where I run to catch my breath, to remember how God saved me, to understand how my story entwines with a greater history, and to remind myself that there can be a way out of no way.

When I feel anxiety rising, I sit, breathe, and picture the room. As if I were Max in *Where the Wild Things Are,* a tree grows up, shading me. I eat of its good and evil, understanding that the world is ripe with bitterness and so I demand the sweetness. I must have the peace. I open myself, lifting my chin in resolute determination of worthiness, unclenching my fingers in a pose of forgiveness, and unfurling my suffering so that it might be exposed to God.

A SEARCH FOR HEALING BEGINS

That room contains the honest answer to the
questions people ask me.

"Why are you still a Christian?"

"Why do you still care about church?"

"Why did you decide to become a minister?"

Yes, Christianity was and is part of the problem,
the cause of much suffering, anxiety, and pain in life;
but Christianity has also been my cure, my solace,
my center. Through the years, I could recognize the
serenity God provided that morning in my room,
and so I've searched to understand that moment of
peace better. I immersed myself in religion. I tried to
figure out what happened through the conservative
Christianity in which I grew up, and so I went to a
Bible school. While there, I became much more aware
of the bitterness, realizing even more that religion
not only heals but can also cause deep suffering. I
discovered the sexism, cringed at the homophobia,
and recoiled at the political maneuverings in the
church that lubricated the rich and damned the poor.

But I knew these problems did not really
represent God. In my longing for a healthier, more
compassionate faith that reflected the God I had met,
I left the conservative church of my youth and became
a part of a progressive tradition. As I learned what
my theology could be, people began to walk alongside

me, encouraging me to study and wrestle even more.
I became Presbyterian (USA), went to seminary,
and found ways to deconstruct and reconstruct how
I understood my religion. When I took each facet
of faith apart and examined it, a whole tradition of
sacred struggle opened up to me. But the reality of
what I discovered in my bedroom many years ago has
never left me.

This journey has slowly evolved into a calling.
I became a pastor. Through all of the study and
conversation in my parish, I found myself seeking
paths of peace for those I served. I wasn't alone with
my religious wounds or in my hunt for spiritual
healing. Other people ached with pain that religion
caused. I began to see patterns in the ways we found
healing and I realized God was calling me to help
people to separate religious wounds from their positive
experiences with God and to restore the latter.

That is how I came to write this book. I wanted
people to discover a safe place where we could
speak honestly about all the bitterness caused by the
church—the blatant sexism, physical abuse, sexual
harm, and emotional manipulation—while finding
a way to hold on to the sweetness and wholeness and
healing the spiritual life can bring.

I'm not interested in defending Christianity. If
someone's wounds from the church are such that
they reject their faith, I will not try to convince

them to come back. The faith has been around for two thousand years, and it flourished without my protection. Not to mention, I found attempts to engage in "apologetics," or a defense of the faith, rarely take complaints seriously. Apologists abound with smug arguments that make you want to avoid eye contact with them at dinner parties, and their clever rationalizations work to evade the real and valid suffering that people endure. Nor am I interested in converting anyone. There are enough people with that mission in life.

My aim is different. I could not walk away from the faith because that is where I found my peace. That is where I met God. I write for those who feel the deep wounds caused by religion and who, like me, want to heal from them. I've walked with those who left church but longed for a way back. I think about friends who tried to break up with God but can't seem to make the split final. I work with people who declare atheism but found themselves backsliding. I talk with men and women who can't help but pray to the very same divinity they wish to deny. There seem to be so many people who want to heal, but they can't figure out where they placed the balm.

Our souls are tender places. We hold our ideals, hopes, wishes, and dreams there. That's why spiritual wounds can feel so devastating. In response to that inflicted pain, we can reject God. We can

grow scabs in order to protect ourselves from
further suffering, so that our souls might not ever
be susceptible to that sort of pain again. But that
will inevitably harden us to the beauty, wonder, and
mystery of God.

There is another way. As we heal, we peel back
those hardened places and allow our souls to be
vulnerable again. We learn to protect ourselves with
wisdom instead of a simple rejection.

Through these pages, I often refer to my stories but
only so you might create your own histories, places,
and metaphors. You will have your own encounters
with God and sources of spiritual healing, which will
look different according to different temperaments—
for some it will be a thoroughly intellectual endeavor,
while others might have a more mystical experience.
Though each person is unique, after decades of
watching people go on this journey, I have found that
spiritual wounds can be grouped into different kinds,
and each has a distinct path for healing. When we
find these paths, we realize that people have been
traveling on them for thousands of years. In fact, at
the heart of the process, we can hear the words of
Jesus:

> Love the Lord your God with all your heart,
> and with all your soul, and with all your mind. . . .
> love your neighbor as yourself.[2]

We practice loving God by healing our image of God. We love ourselves by recovering our emotions, brokenness, and bodies. We love our neighbors through regaining our hope and reassessing our finances. Though a person needs to be actively open to the healing, it is work that begins and ends with God. And that's good news, because no matter what we've learned in moralistic lessons of Sunday school or from the rantings of oily-haired revivalists or the nastiness of venom-filled religious bloggers, God is rooting for us. No matter who we are or what we have done, God is *for us*.[3]

These paths will not open to us because we achieved something, nor will they close because we haven't arrived at some sort of perfection. They are open to those who are open. That is all God requires.

I invite you to hold this book lightly. If you're coming from a more conservative background, as I did, please don't think that you have to believe (or not believe) everything that I do to continue reading the pages. Glean what you can from them, even if that's simply discomfort. If I say something cynical or sarcastic about a belief you hold sacred, I apologize. Much of this is written from my own wounds, and I often handle pain through humor, so I have found that my words can be more biting than I intend.

In these pages, we will acknowledge the pain Christianity causes as we ask God for healing.

Exploring that tender spot, we will lift up the wounds and search for the salve.

FINDING SPACE

Since many of us have learned and internalized damning messages that harmed us over years or even decades, it will take some time, discipline, and practice to relearn faith. We need space to peel back that scab of rejection and apply the ointment of wisdom. I've provided exercises at the end of each chapter, designed to help us open ourselves to God, explore our histories, and recover a sense of wholeness. You may do the exercises alone or with a group.

To begin the process of healing spiritual wounds, you'll need to find a space in which you can do the work. When we need to heal from a substantial physical wound, a nurse will say, "Get some rest." When we recover from a psychological trauma or emotional pain, we are told, "Time will heal." The wisdom extends to healing from religious wounds, because whenever we do any sort of soul work, we need space—not only a physical space but also space in time and emotional energy.

Some of us hardly have sixty seconds to relieve ourselves without kids interrupting the process.

Others work so many hours that we're rarely alone with our thoughts. Yet, in order to do the work of healing, you will need that place where you can open your vulnerable self. It can be a journal where you can work through your thoughts. It can be the place where you walk your dog or the early morning before anyone wakes. But the first thing that you should do is name the place and time. Like an astronaut placing a flag on a barren planet, sometimes you have to go ahead and seize it. Carve out time (thirty minutes to an hour) from your day. Write it down, in the margins of this page, type it into your phone, and declare it in your calendar—your space for healing.

✿ *The Opening Exercise*

Before unfurling stories, reclaiming beliefs, and molding memories, start with a physical posture that is open to God's work. As you begin each exercise, acknowledge God's presence and your willingness.

You can sit, uncross your legs, place your hands on your lap, with palms up. Breathe deeply, imagining that your breath is God's Spirit. It is in God that you live, and move, and have your being.[4] Listen to what your body is saying. Do you feel stress in your neck or muscles? If so, imagine breathing into that part of your body. Stretch it out a bit. Notice any knots in your stomach or pain in your back.

In the space that you have claimed, with your posture of openness, you can pray. When you haven't prayed much or you're out of practice, it can be good to use the words of other people as your guide. I often pray the words of Howard Thurman:

> *Lord, open unto me.*
> *Open unto me—light for my darkness.*
> *Open unto me—courage for my fear.*
> *Open unto me—hope for my despair.*
> *Open unto me—peace for my turmoil.*
> *Open unto me—joy for my sorrow.*
> *Open unto me—strength for my weakness.*
> *Open unto me—wisdom for my confession.*
> *Open unto me—forgiveness for my sins.*
> *Open unto me—love for my hates.*
> *Open unto me—thy Self for* my self.
> *Lord, Lord, open unto me!*
> *Amen.*[5]

Each time you work through the practices, you can begin with the opening exercises, preparing yourself to gently remove that scab.

Chapter 2

FINDING *SHALOM*

I held the clear plastic cup of wine in my hand and watched as my husband, Brian, flitted through the crowd with ease. His animated voice propelled over the beating music, and his enthusiastic arms waved with each word. It was his party and his friends. I was the plus-one tagalong. Still, I admired his charisma. Large gatherings full of loud strangers seemed harder for me. He typically got more anxious than I did, but while his anxiety propelled him outward, meeting and greeting people with energy, mine made me burrow inward.

I decided to rely on my old party trick. I took a deep breath of sweaty, perfumed air and looked around for someone who looked as alone in the crowd as I felt. Surely I could find a fellow introvert. I spotted him, at one corner of the food table, taking way more interest in the cheese assortment than any dairy products warranted.

"Which one's the best?" I asked.

"Well, it depends. Do you like soft or hard cheese?" When I answered, he pointed me to a lovely goat milk and herb concoction that made something inside of me melt. I nodded and hummed in appreciation.

"So, what do you do for a living?" he asked.

I smiled. His opener reminded me that I was in DC. People practically shook hands with business cards up their sleeves. But this bit could be a little awkward, especially when strangers expect a CV filled with political campaigns or NGO designations. Through bites of hors d'oeuvres, they try to suss out governmental codes, such as "GS-14."

"I'm a pastor. And a writer. I lead conferences," I answered.

"You work at *a church*?" He looked confused as he rapidly took inventory of the whole length of me with suspicion. I supposed if I were a casting director, looking for just the right person to play the role of a minister, I would not pick a five-foot-tall curvy woman wearing a T-shirt and jeans.

"Yeah," I said, and smiled, acknowledging his furrowed brow. "Pastors come in all shapes and sizes now. Thank *God*." But then I realized those forehead creases weren't really about me. Something else was going on in his mind.

"Did you grow up in church?" I asked.

He told me about his religious background, and

within moments, the pain in his voice spun this web that entangled all my attention.[1] "My parents were in the military," he said, "so we went from one navy chapel to the next. We weren't really a part of a denomination.

"Then when I was a teenager, we had this chaplain who preached against 'hom-o-sex-uality' every week." He took his time drawing out a Texas accent, mimicking the preacher. "*Every week.* I knew I was gay. There was no denying it." His eyes drifted beyond me, and he fell silent, as he seemed to search for serenity. "I *did* deny it though. I didn't want to be rejected by my family or by God. So for all those years, I rejected myself.

"Can I be honest?" He suddenly focused on my face, reading my brow to see if he could detect those traces of abhorrence he knew well from his youth. I nodded my permission. "I hate Christianity. I *hate* Christianity. It took away my family. Hell, I almost destroyed myself because of it." Our conversation grew silent for a moment, our words got swept up in the surrounding beat as I let the information sink in. Then he persisted. "But even after all of that, I know that unless I make peace with Christianity, I'll never have any peace." He flushed and looked down at his hands, "I'm sorry. I shouldn't go on and on."

"You're good," I said. And then I said it again with gravity, because I believed it and I wanted him to hear me. "You are *good.*"

With a deep breath, he explained how he shifted from feeling shame because of his sexual orientation to a remorseful embarrassment that he could have ever been a Christian. He severed his past from his present, cutting off his Christian upbringing from his life as a gay man. It was the only way he knew to save himself, but it didn't work for long. "Over the years I found out that Christianity was like an appendage. Like an arm or a leg, I couldn't throw it away. If I tried, I was just left with this big hole. Finally, I had to admit that being a Christian was as much a part of me as being gay."

As he spoke, these perplexing words from the Hebrew Bible echoed in my mind:

Come, let us return to the Lord;
for it is God who has torn, and God will heal us;
God has struck down, and God will bind us up.[2]

I can't cram those words into any sort of neat and tidy theological system. They aren't meant to be a divine explanation of who God is; rather, the poetry reflects the cry of an imperfect people. The words give voice to the broken bitterness people feel when wounded, even as they articulate a hope in a God who heals, a God who knows how to clean out the bleeding gashes and bind the lacerations securely enough so that they could recover properly. As I examined the

face of the man next to me, the poetry felt true—not
in a theological sense, but in an existential sense: *God
has torn. God will heal.*

Then, I began seeing things spiritually. Shattered
pieces appeared on the floor of our friend's house—
glistening fragments of this stranger's torn and
struck-down life. The beliefs, relationships, and
yearnings that made up this man felt as acute as
recent wreckage. I longed to put each beautiful piece
together, carefully and delicately. I wanted to embrace
him, surround him, and force him into wholeness. But
I couldn't.

Shalom. Shalom. Shalom. I silently prayed.

Needing some air and a bit of quiet, we walked
outside. Though other members of the party had
already spilled onto the lawn, we were able to find
a suitable green space to continue our conversation.
With each step we took, I continued my prayer.

Shalom—the ancient Hebrew blessing means peace
but it also means wholeness. The word is pliable.
People use it as a greeting or as the goal of treaties
between nations. It also has an economic aspect to it.
The root letters of the Hebrew word can mean "it was
paid for" and so it can be applied to convey a hope for
prosperity. Or it could be used in the way I was using
it—as a meditation, a longing for God to heal.

I told him about my prayer. The word seemed the
only thing I could offer, and so I kept chanting the

intercession in my head, even while recognizing the disorienting force of religion. Systems of beliefs could easily tear at us and break us. The church this man experienced had taken sexism, homophobia, racism, greed, and violence and dressed them up so they appeared as piety. Many of us have met that face of the church.

Yet, even in the midst of these wounds, I couldn't deny that God could heal. I knew that since the tree grew in my room, and I've seen God work similarly in many others' lives. I have witnessed people recover wholeness in the midst of addiction. I have watched people escape the torrents of abuse and find wholeness. I have known enough people on their deathbed to realize that hope shared can build a bridge strong enough to give a person the miraculous courage to cross over to death. And I have seen people who have been wounded by religion's hatred pick up the scattered pieces of their lives and bind them back together. I had seen it happen too many times to deny it. God can heal.

I didn't have any particular wisdom for the stranger. I couldn't make him forget his experience or hand him a self-help book, but I shared and prayed that simple one-word meditation—*shalom*—because it is the best one-word answer to what all hurting people seek and need. That prayer was the one thing we had in common, even if we had to go back to the faith of his youth to retrieve it, and even if that act felt like stealing bandages from the enemy's encampment. With that word, we held something sacred between us—a powerful yearning for his well-being.

A rowdy group of partiers came over and broke up our conversation. So I smiled a wordless farewell to him. He nodded back.

Memories are mysterious. From now on, I hope that stranger will not be able to conjure up those horrifying sermons without the prayer. And I continue to pray that peace attached itself to his recollection so that the pain and messiness of that encounter could begin a journey toward wholeness.

We parted, but the stranger's wisdom lingered. Even though the church caused much of the suffering and violence in his soul, he could not simply walk away from his beliefs. He had nurtured the hardened scab long enough, and he needed to be healed in a way that recognized and incorporated his faith. That was what I wanted to help him with in our brief and stumbling conversation. I heard in his words that he was on a healing journey, that he was seeking to reconnect with God in a new way.

PICKING UP THE SHARDS

Years after that chance encounter, I sensed a larger movement occurring in spiritual circles. It seemed like many of us who were hurt by the church were forging some sort of path toward spiritual healing, whether we bumped into a pastor at a party or sneaked back into a cold, hard pew after a decade of absence. It was a common occurrence.

The wounds were easy to see. People on the Internet hinted at them through status updates with "trigger warnings," soul-baring from new atheists, and tortured blogs of ex-fundamentalists. I worked with the religiously wounded in church and met them at retreats. They were people with the sort of trauma that comes when your injuries are wrapped up in the condemnation of the soul, the shunning of families, or the shaming of flesh.

The lacerations ranged in acuteness. A man revealed a paper cut when he told me about being scolded by a haughty elder lecturing him on his shabby shoes. He knew his parents couldn't afford dress shoes, and so to protect their dignity and his own, he refused to attend church.

Other times, a scar lingered after a woman felt subhuman in her religious community. She chafed with complementarian teachings of obedience and submission in the very place where her full humanity should have been celebrated.

Still in other moments, I witnessed deep gouges inflicted by a manipulative man in his collar seducing a young boy into his forbidden bed. I watched how the abuse did not affect just the boy, but it rippled to his family, friends, and community.

It was staggering to see what people suffered in the name of God. Many sought a cure for their spiritual wounds. They wanted something that made the pain go away or insured that it mended properly. They longed to figure out a way to get back what they had before their faith was damaged. They needed to feel comfortable praying again. Underlying each story, latent questions lingered: *What can I do about this despair? Was this my fault? Where was God when this was happening? Where is the balm to soothe my aching soul? Is God still available to me? Is there any way that I can find healing?*

These questions intrigued me, especially because people asked me—the one who wore a clergy collar— about them. Why would they search for healing in the same place where they were wounded? Why would they be looking to Christianity for a balm?

I knew the answer. Somewhere in my bones I understood. I recognized these moments that ranged from being socially uncomfortable to severely destructive because I lived through them myself. My abusive father regularly used religion to undergird his rage. I also had a pedophile pastor, and I spent my childhood watching as the church maneuvered to cover things up, encouraging parents to forgive instead of pressing charges, and sacrificing victims to the idol of pious pretense.[3]

I've been tempted to abandon God altogether; yet, I stayed.

Why didn't I leave the spiritual life? Why didn't I flee and embrace atheism? Was I like an assaulted spouse who remained inexplicably bound in a relationship that caused brutal pain?

I wasn't afraid to ask the questions or deal with the consequences if I eventually found religion unbearable. It's just that when someone complains of religious wounds, we're often told to quit going to church and disconnect from spiritual practices. No doubt this works for some people, but others see the world through an irremovable religious lens. Asking us to stop believing and practicing would be so unnatural that it would cause certain blindness. It would be like demolishing a musician's piano, breaking an artist's brushes, or denying an engineer's numbers. Some of us have a spiritual or theological orientation, and to eschew that would make us incomplete. Like the wise man at that party, we've found that we need to make amends with our past rather than severing it.

How to make amends is another matter. When I get a physical injury, I know what to do. I can clean out a wound, making sure that the dirt and germs don't infect it. I add ointments and bandages. I know how to Google symptoms. I even have that ability to become extraordinarily paranoid upon seeing all

the horrifying pictures and contemplating the worst
possible scenarios that the hive brain of the Internet
conjures up with my inquiries. To ease my worries,
I take myself to the doctor's office and explain my
physical symptoms. My doctor relies on years of
education to give me the right sort of prescription. If
there is a cure, I will probably buy it.

Psychological injuries can be more difficult to
detect. I used to think that I could make sense of my
psychological conundrums on my own, but I quickly
got in over my head (so to speak), and so I saw a
therapist to work through complex issues, trying to
tease out how I reacted to my family of origin or sort
out my response to a traumatic experience. I needed
someone who knew more than I did about the human
mind, family systems, and how we function, and so I
worked with professionals, intermittently, for a couple
of decades. I learned a great deal by having someone
walk alongside me, listening to my story, and giving
me the tools that I needed to understand my context.

Then I realized this other sort of healing was
needed. It was tangled into the physical and the
psychological, but it was somehow different, because
it was often inflicted by a religious person, culture, or
community and needed a spiritual solution.

Where do we go when we suffer from the sort of
contusions that we hardly have the ability to identify?
What do we do when our therapist doesn't seem to

have the right sort of navigational tools to walk with us on a spiritual journey? How do we heal from that particular religious malaise when we hardly have the vocabulary to articulate what it might be? What happens when we find our vulnerable souls have been wounded, and we don't want to reject God any longer?

This is the space where I work—in this murkiness where the science and labels evade our grasp and give way to mysteries and myth. It's the place where we long for the love of God when we have been taught only of God's vengeance and judgment. We discern the goodness of our desires when we have been told only of their corrupting abilities. We long for the world as it ought to be even when we have been told to pull ourselves up by our own bootstraps. And it's the place where God yearns to meet us.

HOW DOES WOUNDING HAPPEN?

As I wrote in the first chapter, the way we ought to live can be summed up in Jesus's instructions to love God and love our neighbors as ourselves. Jesus said these instructions summarized the entire message of the Law and living by them would be the sign to ourselves and to others whether we were following God. Jesus's words also serve as our foundation when it comes to understanding when spiritual abuse has occurred. Religious wounding occurs when people and communities violate this three-part nature of love—love of God, self, and neighbor.

Implicit in these directives, we understand certain things:

- Jesus commands us to love ourselves.

- The love of God, love of self, and love of others work together.

- Love is generative.

- Love is an act of receiving as well as giving.

- Love can be shown through providing emotional and physical needs.

- Love can also be shown through justice.

- When the Bible contains directives that seem to contradict the law of love, we can assume that those other directives are either wrong or we have misunderstood them.

Imagine these three types of love (God, others, self) as part of a simple machine with three pulleys. The machine works best when all three mechanisms are working. When we love God, we love ourselves; when we love our neighbor, we love God; when we love ourselves, we love our neighbor; and so on.

This seems like an obvious spiritual reality, but it counters what we often think. We imagine love as a limited resource. It's true that most of us cannot manage a thousand best friends or lovers, but we can love God, our neighbor, and ourselves. Doing so generates rather than diminishes love.

We understand the generative nature of love because the command is to love God with all our soul, mind, and strength. After all of that loving, we should be wiped out and completely depleted of affection. But we're not. Even after all that, Jesus keeps talking and says that we are to love our neighbors as we love ourselves.

We might imagine that if we love ourselves too much, then we will become narcissistic and won't be able to love our neighbor. But narcissism typically results from the abuse one experiences as a child and happens when one has not learned to love oneself properly. By contrast, when we learn to love ourselves in a healthy manner, then that love can spill out in excess and we can have the emotional reserves to love others and God.

Parents who lose their temper at a child know that it often has less to do with the child's actual behavior and more to do with the fact that the parents feel hungry, anxious, lonely, or tired. We have not loved ourselves with the necessary provisions, and so we have no more love to give to our children. Love produces love, and spiritual wholeness happens when the finely tuned mechanisms of love work in tandem.

Religious wounding occurs when people and communities violate the love of God, self, and neighbor. This machine of three pulleys stops working and a breakdown happens. For instance, when we fashion a vengeful God who demands eternal torture, we desecrate the love of God. Or when we think that we must hate our gay neighbor in order to love God, then we partake in religious wounding. Or when we imagine that we ought to allow ourselves to be abused in order to love God, then we transgress the laws of love. How do we love our neighbor or ourselves if we think God is ready to torture and kill us if we ever step out of line or fail to conform to God's rules? How do we love God or ourselves if we think it is required to hate others who do not measure up to our religion's standards? How do we love ourselves if we think we must continue to suffer abuse?

For those of us who grew up in a strong religious tradition, we might be able to quote Bible verses that counter these laws of love. Indeed, there are many irreconcilable things in the scripture. That fact may make us feel uncomfortable, but Jesus explained that the laws are made for humans and not the other way around.[4] Then Jesus showed us that certain instructions were wrong when he refused to stone a woman who had been caught cheating on her husband or when he healed the man with the withered hand on the Sabbath—both of which were supposedly against what the Law taught.[5]

In addition, certain texts might be culturally bound to another time and do not apply to ours. For example, laws declare a woman "unclean" when she is menstruating; but in our culture, we know that menstrual blood has nothing to do with whether a woman is clean or not, and we have ways of dealing with this inconvenient week that do not include sitting outside the city walls and not allowing anyone to touch us.[6]

So we learn to hold up certain truths above others as a lens to interpret. And these truths, as Jesus said, summarize the whole of the law—love God, love yourself, and love your neighbor.[7] When religious wounding occurs, it's typically because one of these loving mechanisms broke down; and in order to heal, we can go back and relearn love.

WHAT DOES BEING HEALED LOOK LIKE?

In these matters, *shalom* is not only our prayer, our longing, and our hope, it is also what being healed looks like. Imagine a shattered vase. It will serve as an ongoing metaphor. Throughout this process, we will be reclaiming the pieces of the shattered vase. We will look at the different shards and remnants of our lives—our beliefs, emotions, self-understanding, and practices. We will turn to our past and examine our attitudes toward our bodies and money, and we will do it with the hope of making peace, of allowing all the shattered remains of our own lives to be bound up and repaired.

Shalom may be a different goal than we're used to. In many points in our lives we work for success or happiness. Bookstores are lined with volumes that have those particular ends in mind, and they are both worthy goals, but in striving for professional or financial achievement, we might forget to look around to see how much of the rest of our lives we shattered in the process. Other times, we search for happiness and end up numbing other emotions and so we end up with an elation that lasts about as long as a firecracker before it fizzles.

When searching for spiritual healing, a person might let go of a lucrative job that is destroying her. It can make her feel a whole range of emotions. It's not as if peace will destroy your career or make you sad, but it will compel us to reclaim and embrace things that we tried to avoid in other pursuits.

Finally, *shalom* is not a state of perfection, but a feeling in our gut and a way of responding to the world. Sometimes peace settles upon us unexpectedly, as it did that morning in my bedroom, but that event stands out in my life because it was so rare. Most of the time gathering peace is an intentional process, rather than an item on a checklist or a finish line we will cross. We may work for all of our lives and never achieve a constant peace, but it's an important end for which to strive.

I know that I haven't achieved a state of perfect peace, but I have glimpses of it and I've learned to recognize it. I sense when that cerulean blue settles, when I embrace my past and present and accept who I am. I perceive peace, even when I struggle for justice. And I wake up to it when I sense God's embrace surrounding and holding me.

Through this process, we will learn to look for our own shattered pieces, collect them, and appreciate them. In their sharpness, pain, and brokenness, we will search for ways to put our lives back together. We will make a conscious decision to join that global, historical longing and commit ourselves to that yearning for peace.

WHAT NEEDS HEALING?

I will close with some homework. Below are two exercises I recommend for you to do. Each will help identify what parts of our souls need to be healed and what healing might look like. We begin the process by looking back at the pieces we need to reclaim.

❧ *The Looking-Back Exercise*

Finish these sentences as quickly as you can. If the question doesn't apply to you, then skip it and go on to the next one. Don't spend a lot of time thinking about them until they are complete:

I'm ashamed that I ever believed . . .

When I was growing up, I imagined God as . . .

In church, I learned to dislike . . .

When I went to church, I was embarrassed about . . .

The sermon I remember the most was . . .

The Sunday school lesson I remember the most was . . .

My religious upbringing taught me that I was . . .

In church, I learned to think my body was . . .

In church, I learned that sex was . . .

In church, I learned that women were . . .

In church, people said that being gay was . . .

In church, I learned that suffering was . . .

According to my religious beliefs, I was never allowed to feel . . .

When my neighbors die, they will go to . . .

To God, poor people . . .

I learned that people are poor because . . .

To God, rich people . . .

I learned that people are rich because . . .

My religious beliefs made me afraid of . . .

Look at the answers. As you excavate the things you once believed, you might feel embarrassed and frustrated. Remember that you are identifying a wound on your vulnerable, precious soul, so be gentle with yourself. Take time to forgive yourself. Now spend twenty minutes reflecting. Ask, "How did that belief help me? How did it make me the person I am?" And, "Why did I change?"

We believe things for a reason. Sometimes it's what we were taught to believe, but even those things have a purpose. So we can learn to be tender with our former selves and honor the person we used to be and be thankful for how some of those beliefs and practices led to better ones. For instance, it was very resourceful for me to be a religious kid, because it helped me to be able to pray. Or I often hear people say, "In a way, I'm glad I was so conservative, because I learned to memorize Bible verses and stories."

What did your past religious beliefs do for you? Did they help you navigate a fear of sexuality? Did they give you a sense of safety? Did they give you a good place to go to summer camp or provide a fun youth group? Or did they give you a way to please or connect with your parents?

As you think about your past, imagine gathering the pieces back up and reclaiming them. You don't have to believe them any longer, you can just realize they make up who you are. You were resourceful to believe them at the time. You were resilient. Like growing up in a particular town, you don't have to live there any longer, but you can acknowledge that the town formed you in some unique way.

❧ *Visualizing Healing Exercise*

If we're taking a trip, the journey will usually be more satisfying if we know our destination. Likewise, it's hard to know what healing looks like unless we have an idea of where we want to be. It may be tricky to imagine it, but we've all had glimpses of peace in our past, and it looks different for all of us. In order to imagine where we're going, make a collage. Start with a poster board, a piece of paper, or something you can attach pictures to; then write the words PEACE, HEALING, and WHOLENESS on it. Now look through magazines that showcase visual images and rip or cut out all of the pictures and words that make you think of healing, peace, or wholeness. Again, don't spend a lot of time pondering, but just tear. Arrange the pictures and glue them down.

After the collage is complete, spend twenty minutes writing down what you see. Are there certain locations in the collage that make you think of peace? Why? Is there a certain relationship that makes you feel at ease? What peaceful memory do you recall? Is God in the pictures? Can you locate God? What is your strongest metaphor for God in the collage?

You may find that these torn and broken bits make up a pleasing piece of art, which can be instructive in itself, because it can reflect the beauty that comes out of the process of bonding our torn and ripped parts.

Now put yourself into these images of healing. What else comes to mind when you imagine yourself in a place of peace and wholeness? Can you imagine your life taking on some of these qualities?

Chapter 3

HEALING OUR IMAGE OF GOD

"I had to strip away everything," Pete, a man who visited our congregation, told me over the phone. He wasn't talking about clothes or possessions. He was explaining how his concept of God had to become naked in order for him to walk through the 12 Steps of recovery. "I got to that second step: 'Believe that a Power greater than ourselves could restore us to sanity,' and I didn't think I could do it."

God had not been sane in Pete's mind, and so he couldn't imagine how God could restore him to sanity. Pete was a devout teenager until a pedophile pastor seduced him. "Years after our relationship ended, I couldn't even walk into a church without getting nauseous. I mean physically sick," Pete said. "The name 'Jesus' made me want to throw up. But I had to do the step."

Then Pete realized how Alcoholics Anonymous says "a God of our own choosing," and so he began to imagine God. "I took the most basic definition of God that I could think of: God is love. I tried it out. I lived with it for a couple of days. I realized that I could accept the idea of God if I focused on love. I began saying it in my head: God is love."

Leaving behind Bible stories, doctrines, creeds, and sermons, Pete focused on love. "It became my litmus test. If I remembered that pastor, or thought about hell, or recalled some Bible story that scared me as a kid, I would think, *Does that sound like a loving God?* If it didn't, I threw it out."

I was standing in my office. As Pete spoke, I slid my fingers over the spines of my theological library, carefully curated books I bought with student loans and book allowances, diligently chosen from used bookstores and gleaned at seminary sales. I inherited many from retiring pastors and beloved professors. I've lugged them from apartments to garages to houses to offices across the country. I always knew when I was "home" when my books were in alphabetical order on a shelf—row upon row of intimidating black volumes with the words "Dogmatics," "Systematics," and "Institutes" in the title. I picked up a volume and smelled the yellowed pages, feeling elation. People spent thousands of years trying to understand the mysteries of God. They built

elaborate systems of belief so tightly that to pull one
part of it away would seem to make it all topple.

This thought made me worry. What should I say?
Pete was coming to me for guidance. What did I
think? What if everyone went around, making up
a God of his or her own? Would we end up with
Disneyesque gods that look like the tooth fairy, with
pixie hair and glitter? Or would we construct gods
who look just like us? Do we want a bunch of gods
who took selfies on vacation and spent their time
posting inspirational memes on Facebook? Or would
we indulge in our white military Christian gods with
guns, in an eternal battle with Islam? What would
happen to all that thought and knowledge that made
up my library? God talk is a long, labored discipline. I
had studied theology for seven years and I had barely
scratched the surface. Would we just toss all that out
for our own whims?

Yet I could sense the peace in Pete's voice. I
understood the wisdom he offered. The truth is that
when we describe God, we are always using imperfect
words and metaphors constructed by humans. We're
like toddlers, trying to fit syllables around a concept
so large that our mouths can hardly utter them. Every
time we talk about God, we attempt to know the
unknowable. So if experiencing God means we might
stray from the dogmas of dead white men, I suppose
I could be okay with that, especially since Pete was

returning to such an important realization: God is love.[1] After all, even God invites us to understand God's self that way.

Here is the crux of spiritual healing. The reason religious wounds can cut so deeply is that they carry the weight of God with them. In some way we have felt that God was behind what wounded us. So the first step in spiritual healing is to learn to love God by separating God from our experience of being wounded. Pete had to realize that the pastor who abused him did not really represent Jesus or God as Pete longed to recover a nonabusing view of God.

Focusing on "God is love" worked for Pete. He continued his path to recovery, and though his beliefs would not pass any rigorous orthodox standard, he has stayed sober and he has learned to love and be loved by God. He built a solid relationship with a loving partner. He could even be spotted at church every once in a while.

It was not the first time I heard the story of recovery and reimagining God and it would not be the last. By the third time I heard it, I realized AA held a key, not just for recovery from addictions, but also for spiritual healing. We had to believe in a power greater than ourselves, and for many of us, that meant we had to come to a different understanding of God. We had to learn to love God, which meant beginning a theological journey toward healing.[2]

REFLECTING AND REACTING TO GOD

When we imagine a spiritual path to healing, most of us will not be trying to construct an elaborate dogma or treatise; instead, we're thinking about simple ideas and syllables to describe God. Our idea of God can be crucial, not only for our personal lives, but also for the whole of society. People reflect or react to those we worship. Cultures form around the things we celebrate.

We can see it, on one level, as we value entertainment and art. We give celebrities an honored position, paying them extraordinary homage with money and prestige. Then the rest of us begin to reflect their habits. It becomes a compliment to be compared to a celebrity, and so we mimic their fashion, haircuts, and style. We may not even know that we're doing it, but soon enough, the culture begins to shift toward those we honor.

In much the same way, we value certain aspects of the God we worship. Anthropologists realize this. When students of humankind want to understand a culture, they take a careful look at its religions, myths, and artifacts. A society who worships a wrathful God will reflect violent characteristics and honor those traits in its people. They will begin to believe that God calls them to war rather than forgiveness.

It's not just an anthropological understanding, but it

is also a neurological reality. Worshipping an angry God changes our cerebral chemistry. The amygdala, that primeval bit in the brain that triggers fear and anger, gets a workout when we worship a God of fury; it becomes stronger, and we can begin to reflect that rage.[3]

While reflection is one outcome of our image of God, reaction is another. For instance, when people celebrate a vengeful God who becomes personally violated with every wrong a human commits and gleefully punishes him, people can feel shameful and long for penance. They are never quite convinced that God will forgive them.

A demanding God is not difficult to imagine. The bar is high, particularly when one tries to take a set of laws from an ancient nomadic people and apply them to modern life. The Hebrew Bible puts restrictions on almost every conceivable act—how a person cooks, menstruates, or desires. Then Jesus comes along and in some ways, he raises the bar, telling us that the Law instructed us not to have sex with someone other than our spouse, but Jesus said to not *look* at another person with lust. Jesus could be prone to hyperbole as he preached difficult words, telling people to give away everything they own, let the dead bury the dead, cut off your own hand if it causes you to sin, and deny your mother and father.

If we take every instruction of the Bible literally and universally—as many Christians claim we should—it would be impossible. Opportunities to let God down abound, especially if we imagine God constantly looking over our shoulder with contempt and outrage, waiting for our next blunder.

In reaction to the fear that we disappoint God, we might long for punishment to relieve our guilt, and so we interpret everything as punitive. When we get in a car accident, we are not amazed that we walk away from the damaged vehicle; instead, we look at our smashed bumper and wonder why God is punishing us. When our house is hit by a hurricane, we have clogged arteries, we declare bankruptcy, or we get a divorce, the event takes on cosmic significance and we assume God is teaching us a lesson.

Shame burrows further into us. And then every uncomfortable thing that befalls us happens because we deserve it. Our lives won't be the result of weather, history, or fate. They will be our own failing. God was doing God's job of meting out justice to the deserving. Then we will find ourselves attracting abusive lovers, insulting friends, or harmful religious communities, because we assume that's what we deserve.

Conversely, when we imagine a peaceful, loving God who is for us, we become more peaceful and loving in our actions and reactions. Our lives and our society begin to reflect forgiveness and mercy rather than vengeance and violence. We learn to move and breathe as loved and forgiven people.

IMAGINING GOD

I realized that I needed a healthier view of God when my father was dying. I visited Florida because although my dad had been having a series of small strokes for years, this one seemed particularly worrisome. I arrived at the hospital and walked down the halls. My nose filled with a disinfectant smell that worked overtime to mask the other bodily fluids. When I got to the room marked HOWARD, I entered it, stood at the foot of my father's bed, and watched his closed eyes and steady breathing.

He had a blockage in his carotid artery, and if the blockage traveled to his brain, he could be dead at any moment. The screen beeped beside him as I looked at the glowing green line that tracked the rhythm and flow of his body. My dad had been an engineer at NASA for decades, but he was far from his rocket scientist desk. Now his lifetime of accomplishments and longings, his brilliance and accumulated tangle of emotions and rage—all ended up looking like something that Harold and his purple crayon could scribble across the wall. It was strange to stand before him, watching him with those plastic tubes up his nose.

While completely powerless, he had a sort of peace that he never had when vitality filled his body. All of those years he struggled, and he finally found

contentment flat on his back with a morphine drip.
I watched his even breathing. He looked almost
meditative.

I hadn't cried. It was hard to conjure tears for the
end of someone you feared so much. I wasn't being
disrespectful by saying that he frightened me. He
taught me to be afraid of him.

Dad didn't lift his hand to me as much as he did to
my sister, Leah. He didn't punish me with the dark
and brooding silent treatment that he reserved for
my brother, Mark. Dad stopped physically abusing
my brother when it became clear that Mark could
dominate him in any struggle, but then Dad never
spoke to him. After watching my father interact with
my siblings, sometimes I wondered if I'd rather be hit
than ignored.

I didn't bear the brunt of the abuse, but it still took
its toll on me. In the height of violence, I looked for
ways to stand between my father and the target of his
fury, making peace in any way that I could. I couldn't
always do it though, because sometimes the object
of his wrath was himself. He often muttered suicidal
plans to my mother in front of me.

I knew there was still a connection in my mind
between my angry dad and my idea of God. Even
though I tried hard to exterminate it, it crept up like
a primordial thing out of some swamp in my head.
I suppose it wasn't so strange to have that cognitive

bridge, since I had been praying to "Our Father" every day of my life. In the theology of my youth, a Cosmic Patriarch demanded so much that God would send any random human into eternal torment, and that image had been embedded and highlighted each time I reached back for that patriarchal prayer. Stories, songs, pictures, and repetition reinforced that image of God.

So I prayed, willing myself to conceive a God who was not constructed in the image of the man before me. I closed my eyes and my mind flashed. The Sistine Chapel God outstretched his mighty, white muscular arm. I shook my head, refusing his reach. I heard a quiet hum and looked up at my dad's steady breath.

Walking over to the side of the bed, I picked up my dad's arm. The muscles were mostly gone, replaced by tubes and tape. I patted him, willing compassion and reminding myself, *He can't hurt me. Not now. Not any longer. It's okay to love him.*

Holding the limp hand, I realized that I needed to reconcile with God. Since my father often got angry, and I was taught that my father was my God-ordained authority, I thought that God was abusive and angry with me. I was the problem. I hadn't been good enough, and I shouldn't have provoked him. I was a terrible child. But I was beginning to suspect that the issue was not with me.

MAKING NEW PATHS

Dad didn't die on that trip, so I returned home when he stabilized and realized I had some difficult work to do. I needed to separate God from the abuse in our home and forgive God. My simple machine of love didn't work any longer. A part of it had been corroded from my years of experiencing God as an abusive patriarch. In order to love God, I needed to believe in a loving God, and I had to understand that God loved *me*.

I could comprehend a loving God, on a cerebral level. I made sure that the heavy theological books that sat on my shelf had that much in common, but the message was not getting to my gut. On some emotional level, I was still a child, incredibly afraid of God.

I had to rewire my brain, so that my belly was in on the heady message that God loved me, and so it would be okay to love God. It couldn't happen in the church I served, because in that sanctuary, I was so worried about everyone gathered, it was hard to concentrate on my own work. So I drove to the giant stone structure of the National Cathedral. As I walked past the tourists taking photos under the lintel carvings, everything grew darker and the temperature dropped five degrees. When this place was empty, my heel clacking echoed so much that I walked on tiptoes so I wouldn't disturb the dead. This time a group had gathered for prayer in the center of the sanctuary, so my footsteps seemed to be swallowed up in the other reverberations.

If you think of a cathedral as the shape of a cross, the gathering was clustered at the heart of the beams. The priest and musicians stood as the people formed a "U" shape around them. Since there were plenty of vacant back seats, it was easy for me to slip into one and begin chanting with those gathered without much notice:

> *Bless the Lord, my Soul.*
> *And bless God's holy name.*
> *Bless the Lord, my soul.*
> *Who leads me into life.*[4]

Even if the song were not familiar to me, the melody would soon become easy on my lips. The words repeated, until people began to know their way around the awkward space of the notes, rhythm, pauses, and syllables. Our lips took on the motions of one mouth, and our voices sounded as one voice. The second time through, the more adventurous singers harmonized, taking a couple steps away from the grounding refrain on a parallel track. The third time, they created their own melodies within the larger structure, and layers of beauty bloomed, as sopranos soared to the heights of the grand space.

I looked down at my arm, filled with bumps.
My skin didn't just pucker from the chill that never
seemed to leave the inside of the stone structure; my
flesh felt alive with creation unfolding around me. I
suddenly realized how fleeting live music was. I had to
be fully present, because the notes surrounded me like
ephemeral art that would dissipate into thin air, and
the beauty of its creation became more precious with
the immediacy of the ascending chorus.

I lifted my eyes and searched the faces surrounding
me, even though I felt like I was cheating, like a girl
peeking at her neighbor's test when she should have
been concentrating on her own work. I had to see the
men and women who joined me in this grandeur.

A man, whose pew was situated at a ninety-degree
angle to mine, embodied such contentment that
peace seemed to penetrate and radiate from him. As I
inspected his features, I wasn't gazing at the reflection
on the top of a mucky lake. The shiny surface didn't
hide what lived beneath, but it was a pure stream.
My eyes could see all the way down to the bottom,
as all of his muscles and bones sighed in serenity. It
looked as if he would be perfectly pleased if the chant
continued for three hours.

The woman beside him held a countenance of
longing. Her mouth forced downward in an ancient
yearning that could grace an icon.

Another woman furrowed her brow in concentration as her brain got a tune-up. Maybe she was like me. All of the connections in her head had been corroded, and she worked on rewiring them.

Though the act of singing appeared simple, I knew a complicated healing process had begun—physically and spiritually—as we joined in the repetition. We imagined a compassionate God as we sang our prayer, and through that process we cleared out new paths of life in our minds. The chorus conjured up Jesus's words:

> Enter through the narrow gate; for the gate is wide and the road is easy that leads to destruction, and there are many who take it. For the gate is narrow and the road is hard that leads to life, and there are few who find it.[5]

As a young woman, this passage made me think that God created the world, formed diverse and beautiful creatures from the dust of the earth, and breathed life into them. God fell in love with the creations, delighting in them and promising them they would always be cherished. Then God decided to destroy most of them, unless they happened upon an itty-bitty gate. If they couldn't find the entrance, they would go to hell for an eternity of torture.

What a horrific God. The image perfectly fit my imagined need for punishment.

I looked at this text differently as I longed for a loving God. I could see how easily people venture down destructive paths to rumination. We imagine God as we try to make meaning out of our suffering. We begin on those wide roads with a natural urge to resolve a problem. Suffering stands out in our minds, our attention focuses on pain.[6]

Walking farther down the path, we can backslide from resolving to rehashing, as our minds keep drifting back to the painful experience of trauma or grief. We see how our need to re-create a crisis plays out communally on our television screens. When a tragic event occurs in our country, we watch it on the headline news repeatedly. Much in the way we repeatedly watch a crisis on television as we long to create meaning amid tragedy, we tend to replay damaging personal experiences in our minds over and over again.

Replaying the scene in our minds can often have positive results. It can help us learn how to respond better the next time it happens, or it might help us to find some purpose or meaning in our pain. It can become destructive when we relive abuse in our minds until we begin to be convinced that we deserved the mistreatment. Tragically, we can continue our journey farther down that destructive road if we look for ways to reenact violence in our lives.

The wide path from remembering to rumination

becomes even more complicated when the cruelty comes from religion. The brutal message that a man was an abomination to God because of his sexual orientation became a wide, destructive path my new friend at the party could revisit with ease. Thirty years later, he could recall the exact wording of those sermons from his youth, even though we don't remember most sermons past lunch. He had no problem recalling the toxic words because they had become well-worn trails of hatred, bitterness, and resentment. Wide is the path to destruction.

Pete had been holding the guilt of his relationship with his pastor for so many years that he also created a well-worn, destructive path as he could not untangle the sexual predator from his beliefs.

Hovering in the shadows of abuse and thinking it was God's intention for me to bear it was my destructive path. I had to find the narrow gate and some sort of life-giving message. I had to find new paths that lead to a more compassionate faith.

The path to destruction was wide for me, but the liturgy opened a way, coaxing me from my ruts of victimhood and opening up new avenues of life. The beauty of the prayers had been crafted for thousands of years, because those who tend to the spiritual life understand what our souls need.

Chanting the words altered my neural pathways,

because repeating a sound or phrase reduced the stress, anxiety, depression, and anger that reliving trauma caused. As I focused on a life-giving God, I cleared away brambles and bushes. Limbs scratched my face, but I kept walking until the soil beneath us became packed down and hard. With the reiteration, the path became clear in my brain, so it would be easier to return to when I needed it. The music deepened the emotional experience and sharpened my attention.

The chant was from France and had been sung all over the globe, which reminded me of how the act of meditating alongside others could be powerful because the evolutionary process made it so that our human brains resonate with the emotional states of those surrounding us. So, when we create a path of life in our own minds, we can invite others to share the road. These paths—when they're formed with ancient songs, liturgies, and scripture—are intensely personal *and* communal.

Hearing the familiar chants, listening to venerable liturgies, repeating well-worn scriptures in our minds rewires our brains in the same ways that imagining an angry God does. It gives us another trail to walk down—one with healing and ancient promises, passed down like an old woman embracing us and whispering the peace to each of us.

LOVING GOD

That's what I imagine now, when I think about God.
After I stood before my father and prayed the songs of
life, I asked God for another glimpse. We will never
understand the fullness of God, even when we spend
our whole lives trying, but I needed another image
than the one that had been haunting me. I needed
something just as real as "Our Father." So I prayed,
and then I dreamed.

In my sleep, I saw a small house on the bayside
of Rhode Island (the holiest of places for me). It was
cool, the sort of day that had a rousing edge to it,
but didn't make me shiver. Like a child in a fairy
tale, I entered the home without knocking, and
an old woman greeted me, her round body full of
expectation and laughter.

Although I didn't recognize her, she welcomed me
as if she had known me before I was born. She felt
like a great wise aunt, whom I had never met, but had
kept track of me all of my life. I had the sense that she
had peppered my mother with questions about my
childhood and had a file somewhere, full of clippings
with every article I had ever written. And just as she
knew all about me, she seemed to understand that I
would be coming.

She hardly stopped the domestic chores while I was
there, except for this one moment, when she embraced

me. She held me like I was precious to her, as if she was so overcome with pride and love for me that she could not keep it to herself. As her nose burrowed into the top of my head, I sank into her, becoming a part of her.

Then she let go, and I was my own person, wholly separate. Except that embrace lingered about me, somehow. It felt familiar, even though this woman was strange. It was an enfolding love that felt as if it would consume me, but never did.

Our visit was short, and when I began to leave, she did not say goodbye or see me to the door. She kept washing the dishes and tidying up. But she called out to me, just before I stepped over the threshold. When I turned around, she tossed something to me.

I fumbled to catch it. When I looked down, it was a teacup. It was painted green, the ordinary color of moss, earth, and living things, and it was rimmed with gold. I was shocked that she threw it at me, as if it were made of Melmac instead of precious porcelain. I looked up with wide eyes and she laughed again.

She was my crone, a wise woman who was somehow a part of me, and somehow fully separate. She was also my telos, my goal, and the embodiment of who I wanted to become. I think she was also God, or at least the embrace was God.

I woke up and went about my days, bumping into that embrace at every turn, laughing as I did. About

a week later, I was in England. In the basement of
another great cathedral, there was a gift shop, where
I found a green teacup rimmed with gold. I bought it
immediately and held it gingerly, as if it were a most
precious gift.

When I got back home, I went to the hardware
store and bought a special hook for my mug. Screwing
it into the top of the shelf, I wanted to be sure that it
would be set apart from the chips and clatter of the
everyday coffee mugs, but still within reach. I take
it from the cabinet often and use it. I look through
the thin porcelain, admire its green hue, and sip tea
from its painted edge. Though treasured, I want it
to remain commonplace, as my reminder of that
embrace.

As I consume the warmth of the drink, I remember
how God has led me through dark valleys, through
narrow gates, into the paths of life. And I inhale,
remembering God, the love that embraces me and
gives me life.

RECLAIMING GOD

Often, we reflect or react to God, without realizing
what formed our understanding of God. Sometimes
our abusive experiences forged our divine images,
because we thought that God was the force behind

the harm instead of realizing that God was being
wounded alongside us. God's part in our abuse was
suffering in solidarity with us. Now, God loves us,
weeps for us, and longs to heal us.

The goal of spiritual healing in this area is to learn
to love and be loved by God. In order to do that, we
need to identify harmful images, reclaim a loving
understanding, and deepen our connection with God.
This process may take you a few moments or a few
decades, but it is at the heart of healing, so take as
little or as much time as you need. Feel free to keep
going in the book before you feel like you've gotten
through this step. Most of us will spend a lifetime
learning how to understand and love God.

Begin by opening yourself to God, meditating
and praying, as we learned to do in the first chapter,
so that our vulnerable souls might be open to new
wisdom.

🌺 *Identifying Images of God Exercise*

We all carry a hodgepodge of images of God we have
gathered from religious teachers, family members,
Bible stories, and experiences. Take out a few pieces of
paper or your journal and explore your ideas of God.
Can you recall what God looked like in your Sunday
school stories, church architecture, or religious

paintings? What color was God? How did God make you feel?

If you had a negative, judgmental, or angry image of God, draw God. You can use a crayon or your least dominant hand, if that puts you into a child's frame of mind. Once you have that image, understand that it is the idol that you created when you were younger. Comfort yourself and decide what you want to do with the rendering. You can burn it, throw it away, or put it in a treasured box. Whatever you decide, meditate on First Corinthians as you make a space for a loving God:

> When I was a child, I spoke like a child, I thought like a child, I reasoned like a child; when I became an adult, I put an end to childish ways. For now we see in a mirror, dimly, but then we will see face to face. Now I know only in part; then I will know fully, even as I have been fully known. And now faith, hope, and love abide, these three; and the greatest of these is love.[7]

Replacing Idols with Icons Exercise

The difference between an idol and an icon is that an idol is a representation of a false god and an icon points us to a loving God. For many of us, our childhood picture of God represents a false idol. Now that we have identified our idols, we can begin to fashion an icon, by asking, "What points us to a loving God?"

What is your image of God like now? Has it changed since you were a child? Can you draw or describe God? Can you think of an existing icon that bears witness to a loving God? Is there a person of the Trinity (Father, Son, Holy Spirit, or Creator, Liberator, Sustainer) whom you pray to the most? Why do you relate to that person?

If you have difficulty with this exercise, then pray that the Spirit will reveal God to you in some way. Remember, this process begins and ends with God. God surrounds and embraces you. You don't need to conjure God; you simply need to find ways to awaken to God's presence and deepen your connection.

Recovering Our Theological Shards Exercise

Remember that broken vase? In this part of the healing process, as we long for wholeness, we are recovering our relationship with God, which may have been shattered when we were wounded.

That ancient letter said that "we see in a mirror, dimly." In other words, we usually have mediated experiences through which we can capture only a glimpse of God. Often God's presence is understood through creation or actions, and the way to God is diverse. As you recover your theological shards, you will want to find the ways you experience God.

Can you recover your union with God through creation? Go on a walk, if you're able. Look around, particularly at the elements that surround you, and finish these sentences.

God is like air, because . . .

God is like fire, because . . .

God is like the ground, because . . .

God is like water, because . . .

Pay attention to the birds singing and the wind blowing. Spend a moment listening for God. Is it the rhythm of your feet connecting you to the Ground of All Being? Do you awaken to God through beauty?

If you're not used to doing this, or if you have always been suspicious of people who claim that they have a direct connection with God, listening for God might make you nervous. It's okay. You're not trying to hear an audible voice or create a divine hotline. You are simply trying to wake up to God surrounding you by creating or affirming the ways you connect with that holy presence.

Creation is not the only way to create a path to

God. The way that leads to life is as varied as humans are. What incites awe in you? Is it your intuition and wisdom? Is it through loving and being loved? Is it in church, singing and praying in community? Is it through intellectual challenge? Is it through creating? Is it in reading or studying holy texts? Identify the things that make you most aware of God. Write them down.

When you have found what makes you most alive to God's presence—walking, meditating, loving, creating, learning, singing, or whatever— then intentionally practice these things. Even if the acts seem too fun or a waste of time, know that an important healing process is taking place as you learn to love God and feel loved by God.

Chapter 4

RECOVERING OUR EMOTIONS

I hadn't seen Bruce for over a year, until we were suddenly in a line together breathing in robust beans, waiting for our coffee orders. Bruce was a social worker whom I often reached out to when I needed resources in the community that were beyond my capabilities. But it had been awhile since I had contacted him and I missed him, so I asked if he'd join me for lunch the next week. He declined. He had to go to a meeting. So I asked about another day, and he said he had a meeting.

"You have a meeting during lunch every day?" I asked suspiciously.

"Well, for the next ninety," he said, and I understood. Bruce was in recovery and he needed to go to his 12-step meetings. Many people starting out often go to ninety meetings in ninety days.

Since we both had some time and he wanted to talk as much as I did, we decided to catch up there, in the coffeehouse. We settled around an old diner table, placing sugar packets under a leg to stabilize it. I toasted him with my mug and congratulated him on his days of sobriety.

He told me what finally pushed him to take the steps. Bruce had a contagious laugh. With dark humor and morose cynicism, he could draw out a story until my sides ached and my eyes dripped with tears. He was the center of every party, because like a skilled comedian, he knew how to push social boundaries until everyone felt so awkward that they had to join in the laughter.

Then Bruce got a job in a Catholic hospital, and he realized that the guffaws were escaping at all the wrong times. The laughter had not been a problem before, because his settings always welcomed a jovial presence. But the laughter was nervous and jangling among the patients.

Bruce's supervisor referred him to a counselor, a no-nonsense nun who immediately asked, "Why are you laughing? There's nothing funny here. Are you laughing at yourself? You're hiding something. That's the only reason for this sort of disconnect. What is it? Are you gay? Are you an alcoholic?"

Bruce was stunned. He went home and thought about the nun's words. He was attracted to his wife and women in general. He had, however, tried to stop drinking and failed several times, and so he decided to take sobriety seriously before he lost his job. The counselor's words, as blunt and troubling as they seemed at first, were an important intervention. They allowed Bruce to dig up the root of his problem—he needed spiritual healing.

Bruce had grown up in a conservative church that taught him that joy was the fruit of the Spirit and the natural outcome of a good Christian life. When people were sad, it was simply because they weren't trusting Jesus enough.

As a child, Bruce had done everything he could to be a good Christian, but that never seemed to help him with his depression. He had been engulfed in certain darkness for years. Since he had been told to go to Jesus rather than seeking psychiatric help, Bruce started self-medicating with alcohol. Drinking was also frowned upon in his church, but it was easier to hide.

When he could no longer keep his drinking a secret, he left the faith of his youth. The drinks numbed his emptiness enough so that he could live with his mental illness, but it also desensitized him. His detachment from the world around him often manifested in inappropriate laughter.

I nodded as he told the story. This hope to numb pain is common. We often reach for ways to deaden our emotions with the expectancy that it will bring us wholeness, but in the process, we go back to denying parts of ourselves. So often, healing from spiritual wounds means that we need to love ourselves by reclaiming and embracing that shard of our emotional life. This may chafe in contrast to our current religion, with its feel-good memes; smug church signs; and wealth, health, and happiness evangelists. Going to God may seem like the last place we'd be allowed to expose our true emotions. At least until we remember that God gave us our full, rich interior life, so it must be okay to inhabit every room of it.

DISCOVERING THE CALLUS

My own tendency to numb my spiritual wounds became apparent when I was in college, where I was removed physically from my abusive home but was often face-to-face with the impacts of the trauma. Since I grew up in a conservative Christian household, with an interest in religion and a longing to help people, in the early '90s, I went to Moody Bible Institute, a fundamentalist school in the heart of Chicago. As part of my core courses, I had to take a class with Dr. Hamm.

Standing stock-still, Hamm's gaze remained fixed just above his students' heads. Most of the professors were impassioned and animated, so Dr. Hamm's rigid cardboard manner stood out as an exception. Hamm looked like a small 1970s throwback, with pants that had no pleats and a big bushy mustache. Somehow he missed the fashion memo. No one had mustaches that year, unless the man was gay.

Hamm was not gay. He was the teacher of the Christian Life and Ethics class, and "ethics" referred to a long list of things that we ought not do. We didn't weigh difficult conundrums. There was no in-depth analysis of Greek thinking, modern ethics, or pragmatics. We didn't study William Frankena, imagine John Rawls's veil of ignorance, or conjure up Michael Walzer's spheres of justice. We didn't study any theories or philosophies. Everything was a straightforward "do" or "don't" in that classroom, and being gay remained solidly in the "don't" column, with so many other things.

If it were World War II and Jews hid in your basement when Nazis came knocking on the door, you would look the Nazis straight in the eye and inform them that you had Jews in your basement. God would supernaturally protect the Jews, because you didn't lie.

That's how it worked in the world according to Hamm. Which meant we spent hour upon hour hearing about what not to do. We must not have an abortion. We must not have sex or engage in "heavy petting."

With that information, the guy behind me began panting and stroking my shoulder blade.

One day, Hamm's topic was marriage and divorce. It was common knowledge that occurrence of divorce was higher among former Moody students than the general population, but Hamm didn't mention that fact. Instead, Dr. Hamm opened up his Bible and read the words of Jesus: ". . . at the beginning [God] made them male and female, And said For this cause shall a man leave father and mother, and shall cleave to his wife: and they twain shall be one flesh. Wherefore they are no more twain, but one flesh. What therefore God hath joined together, let not man put asunder."[1]

Hamm closed the Bible and said, "Divorce is never valid under any circumstance. There is a particular order to the home, just as there is an order to creation. The husband is the head of the household. A husband is to love and protect his wife, and a wife is to submit to her husband. She is his helpmate."

I heard the words, but all I could think was, *Why am I so hot?* I burned up as the heaters kept spewing out their steam. I longed for sleep. My body was shutting down. (Something it still does when I relive trauma.)

I heard the word "submit" often. My father conjured up the incantation on a regular basis. My mother was an author who stole any spare moments to hunch over her small, humming red typewriter. She loved composing books and magazine stories with her brilliant wit, especially when she got to meet famous Christian musicians and celebrities. She relished taking notes on their lives. She accomplished most of her work at home, but sometimes her writing talent allowed her to take exotic trips—like to Hong Kong or Heritage USA.

My father believed in total submission and demanded no-back-talking obedience. He was the head of his house; his word was law.

Yet, in the seventies and eighties, the world no longer worked the same way. Women became a strong economic force outside the home, gaining more independence. Following the civil rights era, teenagers were expected to question authority figures, including their parents. So my strong-willed mother, resolute siblings, and angry father made for an explosive home life. Dad didn't have the ability to keep us in line, and his powerlessness, in turn, made him more abusive.

An ugly montage began to flash in my mind. As small children, my brother and sister would strip down to their bathing suits, stand on the bathroom cabinet, and compare the bruises on their skin in the vanity mirror, a brutal competition to see who got it worse. My father overturned dinner tables filled with food when he was angry at my mother. Grabbing my sister by the throat, he slammed her against the wall as I begged for her life. When I was sixteen, he raged his fists at me while he commanded that I get out of his house.

Like a parent with a tantrum-prone toddler, I tried to learn what would set him off, but there were no set patterns. Later, I would find out he had a borderline personality disorder, or BPD. Though most BPDs are not violent, my dad was, and the diagnosis helped me understand his fear of abandonment and subsequent rage, but I could never quite predict his outbursts.

One time, as a teenager, I confided to our pastor what happened in our home. In response he explained that my father was the head of the household and we needed to submit to him. I repeated desperate scenes with more emotion, yet I sensed that the pastor didn't believe me, and becoming a "hysterical" teenager was not helping my case. My father was charming and a major contributor to the church. And since he was disabled, with a neurological disorder that left the bottom half of his body nearly immobile, perhaps the pastor couldn't imagine it.

The disability did make the violence perplexing, because we all had a bad habit of *not running*. We literally stood there, even as teenagers, in order to receive our punishment.

"You must submit!" my father bellowed at my mother with such guttural determination and disgust that I could not imagine treating my dog in the same manner. And my mom, a good Christian above all else, submitted. She never interfered, unless the loss of life was a clear possibility.

One particularly difficult night, Mark mourned, "The more religious dad gets, the more abusive he gets." It was true. Since dad had quoted Bible verses as his anger ignited, he had ingrained a connection between abuse and religion for both of us.

My swirling thoughts snapped back to Dr. Hamm's classroom when a hand shot up in the air. Someone spoke up—a French woman, an international student. "But what if you are being abused? Are you saying that you cannot divorce your husband if your husband beats you?"

"That's right," Dr. Hamm said, while actually making eye contact for an instant, but his voice didn't intonate as he justified, "If you are being abused, that is your cross to bear."

"But what about children? What if they're being hurt?" the woman asked, her voice rising in a stunned protest. "Are you saying that a mother cannot defend her children?"

After a short pause, Hamm stiffly resolved, "It is their cross to bear as well." I looked at Hamm's face. He had no more emotion than if he explained the inevitable suffering of a blood-sucking tick. Hamm inhaled and glanced at the wall clock. "Now. Let's move on."

The woman crossed her arms and scanned the room for some shared outrage. Nothing. With a second sweep, her eyes had the look of a wild caged animal pleading, *What the hell is wrong with you people?* When she couldn't find any resonance, she slammed her books from the desk to the floor in disgust. But it didn't matter. Dr. Hamm ignored her. And most of the room was asleep.

I looked at her but didn't partake in her fury. I just sat with my numbness.

That's when I discovered the emotional callus. I knew that I ought to have been angry, but I couldn't dissent. I couldn't even move. I had been building up that hard skin for years. I didn't have the hormonal rage that people expected with teenagers. My emotions always seemed to be written out of the drama of our family, like the extraneous babblings of a superfluous character that got red-penciled by the editor.

Hearing these "ethics" explained a lot of things that happened in our home. So I took in Hamm's words but was paralyzed, the result of a little body crushed by that cross it had borne for so many years.

As I watched the back of that student's head, hugging her arms, and breathing deeply, God awoke something in me. I didn't have the student's righteous indignation—yet. But I realized I needed to be roused from my numbness.

REALIZING RELIGIOUS NUMBING

In many ways, we are conditioned for numbness. We sit in climate-controlled rooms, entertain ourselves with mindless distractions, and barely notice our pain before we reach for an aspirin bottle. Yet when we find ourselves numbed by religion or responding to spiritual wounds with denial, we only deepen the injury.

Karl Marx famously called religion the opiate of the masses.[2] Of course, Marx was not giving religion a compliment. He thought that religion's happiness was illusionary and kept us from real happiness.

Many of us know there is a downside to religious numbing. For many people who have suffered religious abuse, we have been taught to ignore our own pain. Our trauma is met with trite clichés. When a victim asks for help or explains his or her situation, good Christians might even try to make the problem go away by discrediting the victim. The tactics come in a variety of forms: gaslighting (diminishing the credibility of the victim by asserting that she is crazy, lying, or cannot be trusted), victim blaming (saying that the victim caused the abuse), and martyrdom (encouraging the victim to carry the abuse as part of a spiritual duty) are among them. I have experienced all of these, all within the church.

To this day, as a grown woman and a minister in

good standing, I still encounter these maneuvers from my colleagues. A pastor might ask me, "Are you *sure* what you experienced was abuse, or was your father just trying to discipline you?"

Since I'm more connected with my anger than I was in college, I get upset when people ask me this. Yet, the prevalence of these questions from people who genuinely care about me makes me realize that many people don't always ask from malicious intent. They're not always trying to protect the perpetrator or patriarchy. Sometimes they just want the terrible experience to go away. They can't bear to face that life could have such suffering or that someone they love could be in pain. Since they cannot erase the actual events for me, they try to deny my memories of them.

Whatever the motivation, the problem with denying the events or inhibiting feelings is that there are two types of emotions. There are core emotions such as anger, sadness, and joy. And there are inhibitory emotions such as guilt, anxiety, and shame. When we experience core emotions, we also experience the release that follows. But the inhibitory emotions block a person from feeling core emotions and thus from feeling the release.[3]

Religion can be an especially powerful inhibiting force, because religious messages so effectively produce guilt and shame. For Bruce, the constant

reminder that joy was a fruit of the Spirit and good
Christians ought to be happy created shame around
his depression. For me, the cycle of abuse, disbelief,
and admonishment took away my access to a full
emotional life. That shard of me had been lost, so I
wasn't able to fully love myself. I needed to reclaim it.

As Christ bearers, we have a suffering God. In order
to witness Jesus's pain, we must be able to whisper the
truth of our own torments and bear witness to one
another's agony.[4] I needed to rip off that emotional
callus, feel my anger, and allow God to heal me.

FACING FRIDA

Soon after I discovered my numbness, I found
someone who helped me to feel those core
emotions. While I was a student at Moody, Steve
Hempel, another student, asked me, "Could you do
something?" He showed me a slip of paper in his
hand. It was an address. "I need you to go see Sue
Duffy. She's a woman in a nursing home. I've been
doing stuff for her—taxes and errands—and I want to
make sure she's taken care of when I leave next year.
Plus, I think you'll like her."

I took the slip of paper with the address. It was on
Oak Street, just a couple of blocks down. I shrugged.
"Sure."

"Actually, to be honest, I think you *need her*," Steve said. I nodded and wondered why my classmate talked about Sue as if she were a therapist rather than a woman who could use a bit of help with her taxes.

About a week later, I walked a few blocks and got to the nursing facility, a tan building in a quiet part of Oak Street. I signed in at the desk and made my way up via the elevator. It was crowded, and as it stopped on each floor it looked as if the door were opening on completely different buildings. There was industrial 1950s gray linoleum tile on one floor and frantic people crowded the lobby. The next time the doors opened, there was fresh tan speckled tile and only a couple of people peacefully waiting for the down elevator. Finally, the doors opened to wood flooring and classical music. It was Sue's floor. I made my way to her room and knocked on her half-open door.

"Come in!" Sue sang.

"Hi," I greeted her. "I'm Carol. Steve sent me." When I reached out my right hand, Sue offered her left, and I took it with both of my hands.

"Oh yes," Sue replied as my eyes took inventory of her room. "Steve is very good at taking care of me. He was worried that he wouldn't be here during tax time next year, so he wanted someone who could see me through all the preparations."

With a quick look, her beautiful works of art enraptured me. There were two paintings with abstract swirls of thick brown paint. The back of her door was covered with cards and postcards from all over the world. She had several well-selected books from authors I didn't know: Dietrich Bonhoeffer, Henri Nouwen, Paul Tillich, Jürgen Moltmann, and Frida Kahlo.

"We don't have any tax stuff to do today though. We've got other work. Carol Moseley Braun is running for office, and I'm going to help her get elected. I am sick and tired of white men running our country. They're running it into the ground. It's time to get a fresh perspective."

I looked down at Sue, suddenly nervous. This was a lot to take in. Sue wanted me to write letters for a Democrat. She was obviously a feminist who clearly stated that she wanted people other than white men to run the country. I mean, it was one thing to want opportunities for women and African Americans, but it sounded like she wanted to *overthrow* white men.

I looked carefully at man-hating Sue, that nasty feminist that I was taught to fear. She looked up at me with her red plastic-rimmed glasses from her hospital bed.

I liked her.

"Okay," I smiled. "What can I do?"

Sue dictated letters to the campaign managers. She explained that she had multiple sclerosis, which limited her energy and ability to travel, but she could reserve Tuesdays and Thursdays to make phone calls for the campaign.

I went to see Sue on most Thursdays. Each week there was a new project. I spent a couple of minutes putting receipts into an envelope for her taxes, and then we would start on the next thing—it might be the political campaign, an MS walkathon, or work for her church. Sue was an elder at Fourth Presbyterian Church, a few blocks away from her nursing home, which meant that she was one of the leaders of the congregation who helped make important decisions and guide it spiritually. I became her hands and feet in a lot of her work.

One afternoon, Sue's door was closed. I knocked on it and slipped into the room. "I'm in a bad mood," Sue warned. "You may not want to be around me today."

Her honesty was jarring, reminding me of how often we evade verbalizing our actual moods, but I slid my backpack off of my arm and moved closer to her bed. "What's going on? Is there anything that I can do?"

"No. Nothing," she answered sharply. "I just found out that I'm losing control of my left hand and I'm angry as hell about it. I lost my dominant hand a few years ago, and I've learned to do almost everything with my left hand. But this morning, I went to make my phone calls and I couldn't push the buttons. God,

I can't believe I'm losing my left hand." We sat for a moment in silence before she asked, "You know Kübler-Ross?"

"Yes," I remembered learning about the stages of grief in my psychology class in high school.

"Well, there aren't really stages of grief. It's not like an obstacle course, but there are a whole lot of symptoms when we experience loss. And grief doesn't just happen when someone dies. It happens with a lot of things. For me, it happens each time I lose the use of one of my limbs. And right now I'm angry. Intensely angry."

"That explains a lot. I mean, about my dad," I mumbled as I thought about my father and his explosive moods. His neurological disorder also caused him to deteriorate, slowly. He trudged along with a cane, but he needed a walker. In fact, if I were my dad, I would have been in a wheelchair long ago. He endured the same things Sue experienced, but even though my father was a brilliant rocket scientist, he lacked Sue's emotional intelligence.

Sue had that ability to survey her psychological terrain and describe what was going on inside of her. She could identify the perplexing landscape of grief and relate each symptom to a dry desert, like when she was not able to make a phone call any longer.

Of course, my father's abuse could not be blamed on his disability, and I didn't need to make any excuses for his behavior, but it always helped when I understood his pain a bit more. And the anger that came with the grief surrounding his disability was a dimension I had never before considered.

"Hand me that book, would you?" Sue asked, pointing her chin at her shelf.

I walked across the room. "Which one?" I asked. "This one?"

"No, the tall, thin red one."

"Frida Kahlo?"

She nodded.

I held the book in my hand and thumbed through to a picture of a woman's back with barbed wire poking through the flesh. I winced, closed the binding, and placed it on Sue's rolling hospital desk. She took her left hand, and smoothed it over the cover. I opened it to the first page and she began to explain how Kahlo had the ability to convey the physical and psychological torment she experienced.

"That's her?" I asked, pointing to the somber eyebrows.

"Yes. She painted incredible self-portraits."

I flipped through each page, confused by the surrealism of Kahlo's head on a deer's body, and moved by the crimson that flowed onto the pages. I wanted to bandage Kahlo's wounds. I needed to remove the barbed wire, clean up the mess, and put some gauze on her torn flesh. I wanted to ensure her safety, but I also wanted to preserve her dignity. It seemed disgraceful for her to be bleeding all over the place like that; yet, she was looking at me straight in the eye, without an ounce of shame. Frida didn't hide.

Sue explained Kahlo's spinal cord injury and how the suffering pages illustrated Sue's own aches. I tried to acknowledge that I heard Sue, but my hum wasn't audible. The burning lump in my throat stopped my sounds. I felt a stabbing ache. Literally. I held my stomach and fought my desperate urge to double over.

Kahlo's pain, Sue's pain, and my father's pain pierced me. Then I realized something else—my own agony. I panicked, like someone who cuts herself and doesn't realize it until she sees blood. *Where had my numbness gone?* I had spent years cultivating that emotional callus. I needed it. It protected me. My anguish poured like petroleum into my stomach as I remembered being that little girl, victim of my father's confusing rage.

I had denied my fear and anger and detached myself from the stories that came with them, ever since that forty-five minutes in my disbelieving pastor's office. I figured that's what a good Christian girl was supposed to do.

Yet, Kahlo's eyes lacerated a boil in me. They drew out the pain and pus that I had been hiding. And somehow when I felt that primal acute ache, the memories came back. The stories that I learned to dutifully deny became my own.

Eventually, I put the book back on the shelf and left Sue to her grief. I walked back to campus, not quite understanding what had just happened. God wanted me to be angry and sad, to feel those emotions that I thought good Christians avoided. Stepping along the crowded streets, the sorrow scared me. It felt like the fictional quicksand from a bad '60s movie, and I worried that the sadness would swallow me whole and I would never be able to escape it.

I began to whisper Psalm 23, the poem I learned as a child:

> *Though I walk through the valley of the shadow of death,*
> *I will fear no evil,*
> *For you are with me.*
> *Your rod and your staff,*
> *They comfort me.*[5]

Taking a strange solace in that small preposition "through," the word allowed me to feel, while trusting that there would be something at the other side of the darkness. I would be altered, but I would get *through* it.

On my way back to campus, I gave myself permission to feel and asked God to show me the way through death's shadows. I resolved that I would not deny my heart's aching by trying to pretend that what

I went through was just a misunderstanding, on my
part. I would not allow myself to imagine that I could
have stopped the wounding, as if it were my fault. And
I would not pretend that it was my Christian duty to
suffer abuse. Instead, I would walk through my dark
valley with my shepherd and feel the force of the pain
to reclaim my emotions and find wholeness.

LEARNING TO FEEL

It took years to learn to habitually express the
sentiments. I still have a difficult time. I bought a
child's refrigerator magnet, which was designed so
that toddlers could identify how they felt before they
had the words for their emotions. The magnet had
two parts. One part had rows of expressions, faces
that conveyed different emotions. The other part was
a tiny frame. Each time I passed through the kitchen,
I tried to identify the emotion I felt. *Was I confused?*
Was I afraid? Was I happy? I had been cut off from
these elementary feelings for so long, that emotions
were no longer an automatic response. I had to ask
myself about them and give myself permission to feel
them.

I went to a therapist who instructed me to
"exercise" my anger. So I took up physical activities,
like woodworking, but I quickly learned that it wasn't

constructive to hammer nails when I was blind with rage. I ended up with a lot of bent nails and throbbing fingers. Also, like any muscle, when the angry parts of our brains get a workout, they get stronger. I needed to feel anger without moving into a pounding cycle of violent rumination. So I learned different techniques.

I began to jog, which let me use the emotional energy to exercise, but as my runs got longer, it also allowed me to spend the energy until I became awash in endorphins. I began to understand what it meant to get *through* the dark valley and realize the release on the other side.

I expressed the heartache through writing bad poetry, rendering difficult paintings, and filling endless journals. I learned to get up each morning and identify the emotions I had learned to stifle. I wrote on the top of a page, "What am I feeling?" and then filled the lines, trying to describe my emotional terrain.

I also found guidance from my faith to help me learn to feel. Even though the church I grew up in had harmed me, I knew that the spiritual tradition I was opening myself up to as an adult held wisdom for me. I prayed the Psalms. The book has been called the "anatomy of the soul," so I read through the poetry, often aloud, and let the anguish of the writers shake my bones.[6] There are imprecatory Psalms, which means they are curses full of violent imagery. They are rarely uttered in church, but I allowed myself to speak them and *feel* them.

I began to learn the structure of the Psalms and to mimic the architecture in my own writing. There was an acknowledgment of God, followed by an emotionally charged complaint. Often, the poet accused God of betrayal or forsakenness. Then, the poetry moved again, to a renewal of trust that things would be okay and God loved us.

As I learned to pray in this way, I imagined myself as a child with a temper, my tantrums would be held and enveloped by the enormous love of God. I recalled that embrace from my dream and imagined feeling the pain within that love. I realized that I didn't have to cut myself off from my core emotions, but I could feel the sadness and anger within a larger context that helped me to understand there would be an end to the dark valley. There would be green grass and smooth waters on the other side.

And, eventually, I got there. It took many years before I was able to cry, awash in the release of tears, like an afternoon rain during a suffocating summer day in the South. I could become angry, then feel a settled contentment. When I stopped trying to dam my emotions and force a shallow happiness, I was able to tap into something deeper and realize an abiding wholeness.

I continued to walk with Bruce on his journey. We

met over coffee and then over the phone as he moved into the emotional discomfort of sobriety. He no longer reaches for a drink when he feels upset. Instead, he simply feels upset. I noticed how over the years, his raucous laughter and dark cynicism have settled to a calm wisdom with a wry twist of humor. When he slips into inappropriate chuckling, that becomes a cue for him to take inventory of his emotional progress.

When I ask him about the process, he explains how he delves into art, poetry, and meditation to feel his pain and happiness. He continues his meetings. A while ago, he understood that his depression wasn't something that he could walk *through,* so he started taking medication.

When I ask if he can describe a key to his emotional health, he says, "I've learned to hold my faith more lightly." He believes in God and nurtures his love for God, but releasing his tight grip on religion helped him to take himself more seriously and become a healthier person. It allowed him to connect with his emotions, maintain his sobriety, and journey on the path to spiritual healing.

EMOTIONAL HEALING

Let's go back to that simple machine metaphor and think about how the love of God, self, and others work together. Imagine someone you dearly love. What would you do if that person was upset? You would probably acknowledge their frustration by asking them, "What's wrong? Why are you angry?" Then you would listen to them and comfort them. Acknowledging, listening, and comforting are signs that you love that person.

Now, what happens when you get upset? Do you acknowledge the pain, listen to your story, and comfort yourself? Because these are all ways you love yourself. If you have been taught (implicitly or explicitly) that God does not approve certain emotions or if you learned to hide your abuse by pretending that nothing happened, then that simple machine of love can no longer work properly.

So far in this process, we thought about how wounding happens and began to identify the pain. We recognized that our traumas often carry the weight of God and we began to untangle a loving God from our harmful experiences. Now, we are working to understand when we have become overprotective, so that we can allow space in our souls to be vulnerable again.

The goal of healing in this chapter is to focus on your emotional health, and to do that, you will acknowledge, listen, and comfort yourself. You can start with a prayer, opening yourself up to God. Then get out your journal or a few pieces of paper.

❧ *Taking Your Emotional Temperature Exercise*

Aside from choosing an emoticon on our Facebook status, many of us don't have a healthy place where we can identify and express our emotions. Yet in order for us to have wholeness, we need to reclaim our emotional shards. You can start to do this by acknowledging your emotions. If you don't have a refrigerator magnet for toddlers, you can find other ways of taking your emotional temperature. Write down how you feel. Whether you use words or drawings, do something that will encourage you to dig down and unearth some of the emotions that you have learned to hide. Each morning, take your emotional temperature, and check in with yourself throughout the day.

❧ *Noticing Emotional Patterns Exercise*

After you've spent some time taking your emotional temperature, are you noticing any patterns of denial or masking? For example, do you feel guilt surrounding certain emotions? Do you try to pretend some feelings don't exist? Do you have a go-to emotion?

Does gender factor into your emotional life? For instance, in some religious circles, "manhood" is so important that men are encouraged to not cry, but anger is related to power, so it is acceptable. As a result, anger becomes a go-to emotional response to sadness, guilt, and fear.

By contrast, "womanhood" encourages gentleness of spirit, and so women try to never get angry. As a result, women may respond to anger by crying. "Manhood" and "womanhood" are not biblical; they are social constructions of our particular culture and society. What *is* biblical is that men and women have a wide range of emotional responses. Angry Jael had her tent peg and sorrowful Jesus had his tears.[7]

In order to pay attention to these tendencies and patterns, finish the following sentences by providing an emotion.

I tend to bury my emotions when I feel . . .

I notice guilt when I feel . . .

I get scared when I feel . . .

The emotion I rely on the most is . . .

I used to think that it was sinful to feel . . .

My parents used to manipulate me with . . .

It is not acceptable for a man to feel . . .

It is not acceptable for a woman to feel . . .

A godly man must be . . .

A godly woman must be . . .

My church used to manipulate me with . . .

God doesn't want me to feel . . .

🌑 *Identifying Emotional Cues Exercise*

When Bruce could not express the sadness he was experiencing, he began to laugh. When I feel the fear of past trauma, I shut down and go to sleep. When we have not had access to our emotions and we learn to mask them, our bodies give us cues—headaches, twitching, hand wringing, stomachaches, hunger, constipation, etc.

Learn to listen for the signals your body communicates. How does your body respond to emotions? For the next week, fill out the first two

When I feel . . .	My body responds with . . .
Sadness	
Anger	
Guilt	
Anxiety	
(Add other emotions)	

columns of this chart, paying attention to your body's cues (leave a third column blank).

❧ *Exercising Emotions*

There are certain instances in which people should feel anger, but they have social pressure not to express it. For example, a woman might become angry in a workplace where she is being harassed or a person of color might feel fury over discrimination, but the people around them will urge them not to complain, protest, or even feel. They might be given spiritual reasons to be nice.

If a person has had a lifetime of this sort of conditioning, then some emotions might not be as accessible. Have you noticed your emotional patterns? Is there an emotion that you learned to mask?

Can you respond to that emotion, by exercising it in healthy ways? Painting, writing, or jogging might be ways to express blocked anger and work through it. Finish the chart that you started. Title the third column "I will exercise my emotions by . . ." and fill it in by trying to identify healthy ways to exercise the emotions you may have been avoiding.

❧ *The Anger Meditation*

As I mentioned earlier, some people have been taught
to rely on anger as the only acceptable response to
a wide range of emotions. The amygdala becomes
stronger the more we feel anger. If you rely on anger
to do the heavy lifting for all of your emotions, then
you can practice a simple meditation.

Sit down, with your back straight and your palms
up. This is a posture of receiving. Close your eyes.
Breathe deeply and concentrate on the air filling your
lungs and on letting it out.

Imagine your anger as a small child. Pick the child
up and place her or him on your lap. Listen to the
child. Hear the complaints, tantrums, and weeping.
Then comfort your anger, with the same love and
gentleness you would use if you were soothing a little
child.[8]

❧ *Praying with the Psalmists Exercise*

Read the Psalms with a highlighter or pen. Notice the
great emotional range of the poetry and highlight the
parts that resonate with you. Go back and read those
portions, memorize them, if you would like.

Now construct your own psalm by using the
literary structure, with your own words.

ACKNOWLEDGE GOD. Just as we open ourselves up to God before our exercises, the psalmists acknowledge God in the beginning of their poetry. Sometimes, it's a quick "Hear my voice, O God." Other times it's a long litany of God's attributes. The poetry also acknowledges the feeling of God's absence. For instance, Psalm 63 begins with

O God, you are my God, I seek you,
My soul thirsts for you;
My flesh faints for you,
As in a dry and weary land where there is no water.

Or Psalm 62 starts with

For God alone my soul waits in silence.

Whether you write about God's presence or absence, acknowledge God.

COMPLAIN TO GOD. The psalmists are full of bitter complaints, reviling their enemies until they often sound downright paranoid. Psalm 38 says:

My friends and companions stand aloof from my affliction,
and my neighbors stand far off.
*   Those who seek my life lay their snares;*
those who seek to hurt me speak of ruin,
and meditate treachery all day long.

Write down your own complaints. If you're angry with God, you can write that too. One psalmist cried, "My God, my God, why have you forsaken me?" and Jesus echoed that bitterness on the cross.

RENEW YOUR TRUST. The Psalms often end with a renewal of trust. Psalm 10 ends with

> *O Lord, you will hear the desire of the meek;*
> *You will strengthen their heart, you will incline your ear*
> *To do justice for the orphan and the oppressed,*
> *So that those from the earth may strike terror no more.*

This is a statement of who God is and what God will do in the future. Think about what your own renewal of trust would sound like. Look back on your Replacing Idols with Icons Exercise from chapter 3. What words or images do you use to declare who God is? In what ways do you trust God? Now revisit the Visualizing Healing Exercise from chapter 2. Can you use the images from your collage to construct your own poetry? Write a renewal of trust.[9]

Chapter 5

REDEEMING OUR BROKEN SELVES

I was speaking at a conference. After the scheduled events, a group of us went out for a beer. I sat next to Doug, and in the course of our conversation we found that we had a lot in common. We had similar backgrounds, we lived near one another, and we had both suffered religious abuse.

When I returned to my office, I got an e-mail from Doug, asking if he could meet me for pastoral care. We met outside, on a nature trail, because I found that the context of winding woods helped when people suffered spiritual abuse.

Doug had been an officer in the army and was a tall, robust man who often intimidated people. He was intelligent, direct, and fit, so I watched as this rare trinity caused other men to size him up, and place themselves below him on the scale of evolved creatures.

The interesting thing about Doug, however, was that he didn't think of himself in the same way others saw him. As our feet steadily paced along the gravel path, he told me about his early years. Doug's father, also a military officer, expected excellence from Doug and drove him relentlessly to be a top student, the best athlete, and the most obedient son. Then in the evenings, Doug's father drank too much and undergirded his lessons with violence.

We watched blue lizards scurry around us as Doug told me how he spent his early adulthood trying to please his dad. He joined the army to mirror his father's career. Growing up in South Carolina, he said that God and country had become mixed up in his mind. After 9/11, he had signed up for duty, imagining that he was going to be part of a holy war. Then, after spending time in the deserts of Afghanistan, he abandoned any sense of moral virtue. He felt like the victim of both God and country. Afghanistan was hell for Doug. While carrying his pack through the heat, he was sure that God had abandoned him in the desert, and that he deserved it.

After his military career ended, Doug took a hard look at his PTSD. As he learned to recover, he had difficulty with intimacy. He would fall deeply in love with women, but then he would feel emotionally pummeled. He confided that he felt trapped in his soldier's body. "If I were someone else, people wouldn't see me like this. They would see the abuse and know that I'm a victim." Doug's sturdy exterior hid the small boy who could never quite defend himself or his mother. It covered up the moral injuries he suffered. His wounds kept him from being able to experience the healthy vulnerability needed for intimacy. Doug walked through life, knowing he was a victim, expecting to always be abused.

As our rhythmic steps continued along the wooden planks, I heard more of his story unfold. I became aware that the most pernicious damage that had been inflicted on Doug had not been the fading bruises from home or the wounds in the desert, but it was Doug's idea of himself. No matter what accolades he received in his life, he always felt like he didn't do enough. As he grew, he internalized his father's criticism, repeated the paternal words in his mind, until he felt thoroughly unworthy of love—even God's love.

Jesus said that we should love our neighbors as we love ourselves, and that command is impossible to follow unless we have love for ourselves. Doug had to learn to untangle his religious nationalism, and in order to find peace after religious abuse he endured, Doug needed to have a different relationship with himself. Like the prodigal son, he had to wake up to the arms of God surrounding him and welcome the truth that he was worthy and beloved.[1]

LEARNING TO LOVE ALL HUMANITY—INCLUDING MYSELF

How one views oneself is a common concern when people are longing for spiritual wholeness. It makes sense. Advertisements swarm us each day, reminding us of what we do not have. They taunt us, like sirens' songs, telling us how much we are lacking, and wooing us to buy more. The average American is exposed to three hundred sixty ads every day, each one designed to ignite a sense of inadequacy and longing.[2] Every hour we are awake, we are told twenty-two times that we are not rich, thin, young, beautiful, ripped, or stylish enough. It's enough to make me think that we just might be suffering a national existential crisis.

Even though our culture has been criticized for being too narcissistic, being overly self-conscious can be a mask one learns to put on to hide damage and abuse. In the midst of all this, our religious understandings don't always help, for in a theological attempt to center God and decenter humanity, churches can feed into disparaging messages.

I saw this problematic religious view firsthand as a young woman in Bible school, preparing for our evangelism class. "Witnessing" was the most excruciating thing we had to do at Moody. I hated talking to strangers, but I did it because I had a deep,

abiding concern that people might spend an eternity
in suffering if I didn't save them. What else could I
do? If people were dying, I had to rescue them.

The school was built to train young people to
evangelize. When we went out to witness, we would
confront people (usually complete strangers) and tell
them: (1) we all deserve to go to hell, (2) Jesus made
a way for us so we don't have to go to hell, and (3)
if they accepted Jesus into their hearts, then they
would not go to hell. In order to seal the deal, to get
them to make a decision to accept Jesus into their
hearts, we would have them pray the Sinner's Prayer
with us and to repeat each line, one at a time, after
us. The prayer had different forms, but it basically
went like this:

Jesus, I know that I have done bad things. I want to
change. Please forgive me. I invite you to come into
my heart and live there for the rest of my life.
Amen.

I never actually got to pray the prayer with anyone;
my conversion count was very low, but I kept trying.
Grief burdened me. In my dorm room, I looked out
my window upon the vast city thinking, *We are all going
to die. Most of us will burn in hell for eternity.*

In my imagination, it was as if a plague had
overtaken Chicago, and I walked down the halls of

the intensive care unit of Cook County Hospital, amongst the decay, piss, and excrement. I was completely alive and healthy because I held a vial of life-giving medicine.

I had to offer that cure—no matter how awkward it felt, no matter how embarrassing—because they would *die* without it. No, it was worse than death. It was eternal suffering.

In my evangelism class at Moody, the professor gave the students a chart to fill in the names and information of those we converted. We were to use it as a survey tool to start conversations. We groaned when we saw it.

"I know. It's terrible," Dr. Fisher, the course professor, said while shaking his head. "You take an evangelism class to *talk* about evangelism, and here I am going to make you actually *do* evangelism." His nostrils flared as he looked up to the ceiling. "Fill out the graph. And I don't want to see your mother's name on this chart. You have to *go out and talk to people.*"

A few days later, my friend Brian, suggested that we go to O'Hare Airport. "It's inside, so we don't have to worry about the weather. Plus, there are all those people waiting for a flight. There's *no way for them to escape us,*" Brian said with mock horror.

I was relieved. Even if the whole outing was a disaster, at least we could laugh about it.

That evening, Brian and I took the elevated train out to O'Hare. I took out the graph, stared at the blank boxes, and sweated with anxiety. The thought of going up to complete strangers and asking those questions terrified me. Brian leaned into my arm and said, "You know, a lot of people just cheat."

"What? Really?" I was shocked.

"Yeah. They just pick random names and fill the graph in," he confided.

The (pre-9/11) minimal security allowed us to get to a gate without actually having an airline ticket. I walked along the gate areas and saw a businessman in his midfifties. I breathed deeply, smiled broadly, and said, "Hi. I'm taking a survey for a class. Can I ask you a few questions?"

"Sure," the man answered. He put down his *Chicago Tribune,* and Brian started wandering a bit, while keeping me in sight. "What's your name?"

"Bob White," he said.

"Hi, Bob, I'm Carol Howard," I said as we shook hands.

"Bob, could you tell me what your religious tradition is?"

He smiled with one half of his mouth and asked suspiciously, "What kind of class is this?"

"Oh," I said, while blood rushed to my head. "Well . . . I'm a student at Moody Bible Institute."

"Ah. Moody," he gave a knowing nod.

I was caught. He knew the survey was a scam.

"I'm Methodist," he answered succinctly.

"Do you believe in God?"

"Ye-esss," he nodded and lifted his eyebrows.

"I said *I'm Methodist.*" He said it slower this time. "Methodists believe in God."

I felt a bit of desperation, even as I smiled winningly. This one was going to be tough. The hardest people to save were the ones who thought they were saved already. "Oh, okay then." I glanced down at the next question. "So, Bob, if you died tonight, do you know where you would spend eternity?"

"I would spend it in heaven. Because Methodists go to heaven too," he said, and an amused smile spread across his face. He still talked slowly, clearly patronizing me with each syllable.

It worked. I felt childish. "Oh. Okay," I said again. Trying to remain perky, even though I could feel my spine melt and my forehead glisten, I wrote "heaven" down on my clipboard, and my mind raced. *What should I do? What should I ask him? How am I going to tell him that he's going to hell and he needs to invite Jesus into his heart? He can't be saved. He's Methodist. They baptize babies. He was probably a victim of pedobaptism himself. How can I tell him how wrong he is?*

Bob was waiting for the next question, but there wasn't really anything else on my sheet to ask him. He said that he believed in God and he was sure that

he was going to heaven. I tried to find something
that would lead to further discussion. I could tell him
he had a nice tie. But he didn't. It was plain blue. I
looked at his fingers and wrists. Was he wearing any
jewelry? A school ring? A watch? Anything? Nothing.

To my chagrin, I began to doubt myself. *Maybe he's
not wrong. Maybe I'm the one who's wrong. Maybe he is going
to heaven. And if he is, that would mean that I could put an
end to this excruciating interview.*

I decided to take his word for it.

"Well, Bob, I think that's it. Thank you so much for
talking with me. I really appreciate your time."

"No problem," he said, and sighed, shook his head,
rolled his eyes, and went back to reading his *Tribune*.

I walked away and hit my brow with the palm of
my hand, breathing, "Idiot. I am such an idiot." In a
moment of self-consciousness, I wondered if Bob saw
my forehead flagellation, then I thought, *Who cares? He
already knows I'm an idiot.*

Brian saw the cue and started moving back toward me.
"What happened?" he asked once we were out of earshot.

I looked up at him in hopeless desperation. "You
say that people cheat on this graph?"

Dr. Fisher predicted that we would feel elated after
witnessing. We walked back to the El and hopped
on the train. On our ride back, I tried to feel the
explosive joy that my professor described, but it never
came to me. I just felt embarrassed.

I kept working on the graph, dutifully honing my evangelism skills, although it seemed more like a long lesson in ridicule and rejection. I would be in a coffeehouse, when I would see a stranger across the crowded room. My eyes were drawn to him like a dog to a raw steak. He looked lonely. I could tell that he needed a friend. I smiled broadly at him. He smiled back, and that was my cue.

I walked over to him. My words oozed with kindness as I asked, "If you died tonight, would you go to heaven?" It always ended awkwardly after that. He thought he was getting lucky, and he was just getting some Jesus.

I soldiered on until I finally settled on the right approach. Instead of the sham survey or my clumsy pickup evangelism, I bought some charcoal and a pad of paper. Then I asked people if I could draw their faces. I wanted to practice sketching portraits and I needed models. It was actually the truth, and people responded well when they had the time, especially when I told them that they could have the rendering for free if they wanted them.

We would sit down, in a crowded café or on the front stairs of a limestone building, and I would try to capture the curve of their chin, the weariness of their eyes, the kind corners of their mouths. They would ask me where I was studying, and I would tell them my story. They, in turn, would point out their own spiritual paths. I would continue to sketch. There was something about the lack of eye contact plus the piercing attention that freed people to speak. It was an invitation, like driving a mercurial teenager around in a car. As I drew with my charcoal, it drew them out and made them eager to fill the empty air with syllables. I never got anyone to say the Sinner's Prayer. Instead, I learned to see people and feel empathy for strangers. I began to walk into a room and survey the faces of strangers.

God, she looks depressed. I wonder why she's so depressed.

Why exactly is that woman so beautiful? She's radiating. She doesn't have a classic facial structure. It's like some sort of elegant energy.

He's guilty. He carries regret in his gait. That man needs some peace.

When I settled in with my tools, I began to listen on some subterranean level, hearing things with my ears and my gut. I became aware of our paralanguage. I honed my intuition, swallowed my introversion, and learned to forge connections with people.

I eventually filled out the blanks in the chart, which made me feel like a miserable failure. I had no converts, and I wondered if I could get an "F" in evangelism.

When I got back to my room, I thumbed through the rejected sketches, remembering the smiles and the stories of each person. I had gotten better at drawing them. Though I had not added a single notch to my evangelism belt, I did learn to see people. Waitresses, clerks, and patrons were no longer extras in my life's drama. Instead they became three-dimensional solid beings on their own. They became characters independent of my religious intentions for them or my need to control their fate. They were people weighted with entire histories of love, loss, passion, and betrayal.

Then it hit me. Through the *practice* of evangelism, I realized I was hurting people with the *premise* of my evangelism. I thought we all deserved to go to hell. I imagined an eternal torture worse than solitary confinement for people who were basically trying to live decent lives. I tried to conjure hell in my mind. What would it be like? Probably like the ovens at Auschwitz, but the person would never fully burn.

I felt nauseous. *I thought that people deserved the ovens at Auschwitz when they didn't believe the way that I did.* Did my theology lead me to a worse view of humanity than Adolf Hitler's? I shook my head and held the sketchpad closely to my chest as I tried to make sense of it.

I believed that God would send these beautiful people to eternal suffering unless they repeated the magic words after me. If I loved them, after fifteen minutes of noticing the curve of their cheeks and the angle of their nose, wouldn't God love them more? Or

was God's wrath so violent that it caused some sort
of divine blindness? If God created them, and blew
breath into them, why would God care about that
prayer, that random recipe for salvation? And what
did I really believe about people if I thought that we
all deserved eternal burning?

I had learned to create lovely portraits of strangers,
but they didn't match what I thought about them
when I looked through the eyes of my faith. There
was something horrible about the way I portrayed
humanity in my belief system, which meant there was
something marred about how I thought about myself.

In my panic, the Spirit nudged me to love
humanity—including myself.

RECOVERING HEALTHY METAPHORS

As the decades went on, I worked with more people
like Doug, who felt cut off from God and unworthy
of love. I realized that the expectation that a person
deserves hell deeply affects how we view ourselves
and treat one another. It robs us of our dignity, severs
us from our common humanity, and ruptures our
relationship with God.

I also began to understand the power of what
occurs between our thoughts, feelings, and behaviors.
With the encouragement of a couple of social workers

in our congregation, I studied cognitive behavioral therapy in light of religious abuse.

In many churches, those damnable messages are loud, clear, and constant. When we talk about how humanity needs to be saved, we gather together to sing "Amazing Grace." It's a lovely sentiment about God overall, but it's not such a great picture of humanity, as we belt out that we are wretches. We read passages that say we are worms. The most famous sermon in the United States is "Sinners in the Hands of an Angry God," where a pastor, Jonathan Edwards, conjures up intricate images of a spider being held over a burning flame. We are insects, and God is a maniacal boy, waiting to singe us.

The denigrating images our religious traditions can inflict on people can move us to imagine ourselves as lowly creatures, undeserving of God's love. Small children sit in pews, with combed hair and swinging legs that cannot touch the ground, and are suddenly told that their little bodies will burn in hell for eternity. Much of this belief system was designed to highlight the grace of God, but it is unnecessary to make a creature look bad in order for a Creator to look better.

People who have been wounded by religion have often been given messages that they replay in their minds constantly. They instantly recall a hurtful sermon that they heard when they were small children thirty years after the fact.

In a scriptural context, we can think of these messages as a blessing or a curse.[3] There was a sense in ancient cultures that our words had power, and a blessing or a curse seemed to be weighted with a bit of magic.[4] We have lost that mythical understanding, but the power of the blessing and the curse still remain. When a child is told that he will never amount to anything, then that child lives with that curse; it plays in his brain and affects his emotions and his behavior. When a person understands herself as a victim, she sees the world through the eyes of a victim and behaves as a victim.

One of the challenges of religious healing is to identify those messages that affect our emotions and behavior and to learn new thoughts. One of the most powerful ways of understanding ourselves differently is through positive metaphors.

Metaphor understands that particular words should not always be exact or comprehensive when it comes to explaining things that are ethereal. With metaphor, we realize the limits of our own words, and we struggle to describe realities that do not have one-to-one correlations. We also use metaphor to put a tangible substance onto intangible perspectives.

Since the language that some of us heard in church could mar us, part of the spiritual art of healing will be redefining ourselves by something concrete, a metaphor that calls out strength, courage, or love in our being.

The metaphors of scripture seem endless—lion, stone, rock, devouring fire, dream, flood, warrior, plant, cedar, pot, moth, broken pottery, shadow, withering flower, olive tree, dove, sharp razor, thief, broken vessel, arrow, and breath. We can use these biblical examples. When we muster up metaphors of strength, we can begin to think of ourselves as a reed that bends in the wind but cannot be broken, or a roaring lion in the face of hardship. Understanding metaphors of strength can help us to identify something within us and call out those qualities.

Then we can speak to ourselves in the second person, a practice that made me feel absurd at first, but it's only going on in our heads and it has been proven to decrease anxiety: "Carol, you are a rock. You can withstand the storms surrounding you."[5]

I began calling myself "rock" when I was about thirty and everything seemed to be crumbling around me—my job and my marriage. Then I went through an early miscarriage. I felt the life drain from my body, along with my hope for a second child. My father's condition was worsening. When I went on a walk, I ruminated on all my failures and felt the traumas throughout my body.

I felt the pain of the miscarriage in my belly. I carried the exhaustion from serving my parish on my shoulders. My eye twitched with stress. The abuse along with the anticipated death of my dad made my arms tremor with the emptiness of an unloved child who longed to be held.

My body reverberated with loss until every part of me trembled. I began to pray, asking God for strength. As I uttered my pleas, I looked down at the falling leaves and saw a bird, a tiny nestling, shaking. I knelt, placed two fingers lightly on her back, and felt her quavering. With that touch, I became her. It was the frailty, I suppose, and the fact that we were both shaking. I imagined the tumble from the nest and the inability to fly. I sensed her weakness, the feeling of being a victim of everything around me. It was the weariness that convinced me that gravity itself was working against me. I couldn't bear all the things that I was supposed to be doing, and so I knelt on the ground with her and became that tiny thing. I felt connection with this creature, as real as when a simile becomes a metaphor. Holding my stomach, I felt vulnerability that had been caught up in my bones, the fragility that wouldn't allow me to stop shivering.

I'm not sure how long I was there, on the wooded ground. I seemed to slip into a space where time no longer worked in the same way. Eventually, I knew I had to leave her. When I got up, my knees creaked and ached. I felt the Spirit guiding me as I walked farther through the woods until I got to a beach. The bay glistened with the pure sunlight. The strength of it began to fill me with warmth, and I felt my trembling arms still.

There, on the beach, stones scattered along the shore. And my body took on another urge that seemed to be beyond my own volition. I began stacking the rocks, one on top of the other. I carried small stones and large ones, placing them into an intricate puzzle so that they would stand upright. The rocks felt much heavier than I could bear, but I began to pulse with adrenaline. It pumped into my veins and I grew stronger as I heaved the dense rocks and heard the satisfying hammer of stone crashing stone.

While stacking, I thought about Jacob, the patriarch from the Hebrew Bible, who wrestled with God and underwent a divine name change. He also built a stone altar.[6] When the sweat began to bead on my skin, I recalled Peter, the disciple whose name meant "rock" and how the church was built upon his words.[7]

As I heaved one stone upon the other, God changed my name from victim to survivor. And just as I had become that bird, that shaking victim, I became the boulders, survivors of a thousand years of weather. I joined that strong wall of people throughout Christianity, who were transformed by God, our rock and our salvation.[8] God was among the rocks and in my recovery, calling out the strength in me.

When I was done with the pile, I noticed the sun setting. Breathless, I sat beside my impromptu monument and watched the blazing beauty sinking

across the bay. God didn't let the sun go out like
a light. No, there was this extravagant show of
brilliant color. The neon streaks convinced me that
God was showing off. My altar turned rosy, and
at that moment, my puny pile took on the spiritual
significance of the magnificent Stonehenge. I stood
up, crossed my strong arms, and headed on the path
home.

When I got to the place where my soul had been
shivering, I looked into the trees and spotted my
nestling, sturdy and jumping from limb to limb.

Years after God changed my name from nestling
to rock, from victim to survivor, I walked with Doug
along the nature trail. I held the memories of that
day as I silently spotted the birds and rocks along the
way. I also noticed the curve of Doug's cheek and
the complex history in his eyes. I listened to what
Doug had been told by his father, his church, and his
military training. I sensed what he had been telling
himself. He needed to recast himself in his play. He
needed a whole new character in his drama. God was
longing to rename him.

"Pick out a metaphor for yourself," I said. "You
need a new one. Your old one is all crushed, worn,
and damaged. Can you pray about that? As we walk,
can you open yourself up to what God might be
calling you?"

We walked in silence for a while. Then Doug

named Bible characters he loved as a kid, but none of them quite fit. He looked at the woods around us. Nothing surrounding us inspired him. Then he settled on a ball of glass in a blower's fire. It was in a form that could not be crushed, and had strength in its flexibility.

I smiled. That was it. That molten glass was Doug. God had given him a new name, and with it, he was finally seeing the strength that we all saw in him.

🍂 Finding a New Identity

Now, for our homework. Remember that spiritual wounding happens when that simple machine becomes jammed, when the love of God, love of self, and love of neighbor do not work together smoothly any longer. In this chapter, we are focusing on loving ourselves, by reaffirming God's love for us. The goal of spiritual healing as we recover the shards of our broken selves is to understand ourselves differently, especially in relation to God. To do that, we will claim God's love and learn a new name.

You can begin by opening yourself to God. Through breathing, think about inhaling God's spirit. Pray the words of Howard Thurman from chapter 1, if they are helpful:

Lord, open unto me.

Open unto me—light for my darkness.

Open unto me—courage for my fear.

Open unto me—hope for my despair.

Open unto me—peace for my turmoil.

Open unto me—joy for my sorrow.

Open unto me—strength for my weakness.

Open unto me—wisdom for my confession.

Open unto me—forgiveness for my sins.

Open unto me—love for my hates.

Open unto me—thy Self for my self.

Lord, Lord, open unto me!

Amen.

Claiming God's Love Exercise

You can understand yourself in relation to God. Sit down with two blank pieces of paper. On each line of page 1, write those words that rumbled from the heavens when Jesus was baptized, but place yourself in the sentence:

"I, (your full name), am God's (son/daughter/child), the beloved. God is well pleased with me."[9]

Repeat the sentence until you fill the page. As you write, you might hear yourself arguing with the statement. "Who do you think you are?" something inside of you

may chide. "You're gay! How could God love you?" Or
"That's ridiculous. You don't deserve God's love. You're
a slut!" Or, "If God really loved you, then that terrible
thing would have never happened to you!"

When you hear those protests, write them down
on the second sheet of paper. If you hear the same
disagreeable statement ringing in your ears more
than once, then write it down more than once. Then
turn to page 1 again and keep writing how you are a
beloved child of God, until you fill the first page.

Look at the arguments. Where did the protests
originate? Can you identify when and where you first
heard them? Has someone been blocking you from
God's love? Take some time to journal or talk with
a friend about what statements are keeping you from
fully receiving God's love.

As you think about the experience, can you have
compassion for the person who said these things to
you? Can you imagine how difficult it must have been
for that person to live with such a judgmental God?
Can you forgive the person who said it?

Can you forgive yourself for that thing that is
keeping you from God's love?[10] Read Romans 8:38–
39: "For I am convinced that neither death, nor life,
nor angels, nor rulers, nor things present, nor things
to come, nor powers, nor height, nor depth, nor
anything else in all creation will be able to separate us
from the love of God in Christ Jesus our Lord."

Now, look at your page of false statements and think about what you would like to do with them. Can you create a ritual around getting rid of them? You can rip them up or light them on fire. You can sing, light candles, burn incense, or practice smudging as you get rid of them. Or, if you talked to a friend about the process, then you can invite him or her to witness the disposal.

Each time you hear water running, remind yourself, "I am God's child. The Beloved. God is well pleased with me." If you're standing in front of a mirror, getting ready to brush your teeth, look at yourself as you say it. This will remind you of your baptism (if you've been baptized), and it will remind you that God's love is unconditional.

🌹 *Finding Your Metaphor Exercise*

Either go on a walk, journal, or set aside time for silent meditation—whatever form of prayer makes the most sense to you. Then ask God for a metaphor. It might be something that comes from a Bible verse, or a character in the Bible, or a song you sang in church. It might be something from nature, or it might be a mythological creature. You may think of something quickly, but you don't fully understand it. That's okay. When you get a chance, you can research it more fully. Write down your metaphor.

When you figure out what resonates, then begin to call yourself by that metaphor. "Carol, you are a rock." These second-person affirmations will feel uncomfortable. But they're powerful tools to build resilience.

Chapter 6

RECLAIMING OUR BODIES

The text came late at night.

> Carol? It's Barbara.
>
> > *Hey. What's up?*
>
> Sorry to text so late.
>
> I'm scared. Need to talk.
>
> Tomorrow?
>
> > *Of course.*
> >
> > *Do you need to talk now?*
> >
> > *I have time.*
>
> No. Can't.

As I negotiated the time and details with Barbara, a neighbor I met at a block party, the urgency became clearer. I don't know how to sense tears with a smartphone. Grown-ups who are really crying don't use the little yellow emojis. But somehow those digital letters looked desperate.

We met at my home. Barbara was supposed to be at work but called in sick. When I saw her, I realized she was telling the truth. She looked ill, pale with the sort of puffiness in her eyes that comes from weeks of sorrow.

"What is it?" I awkwardly side-hugged her while handing her a mug of coffee. We sat down.

"I've been having an affair. I told my husband and ended the relationship," she said, dumping the news like a mountain of stones she was too tired to carry any longer. I nodded. "But now I'm not sure what's going to happen with our marriage. Or with me."

Barbara was not a churchgoer, but it didn't matter. Even when you're used to sleeping in on Sunday morning, most people need a confessor at some point in their lives. In my tradition, we don't believe in confessing to priests. We don't think that there should be an intermediary between a person and God, but that doesn't keep it from happening on a practical level. Sometimes a person feels like she can't really face God alone and she needs someone standing with her.

The story tumbled out. A flirtation in the office became lunch. Lunch became an affair. It was really fun, until it began crushing Barbara. She was in an elevator, and she thought she was running out of oxygen. When the door opened, she ran out of the enclosed space and began gasping.

As Barbara told me this, I imagined a snake wrapping himself around her neck. Then I noticed my arms and legs, and uncrossed them. I arranged my face into an open, nonjudgmental expression. She didn't need me heaping any shame on her. She was clearly soaking in it.

After a few moments, she was done with her story and sat, fingers trembling in her lap. She stared at them as if she could will them to stillness with her eyes.

"Barbara, we can do a ritual. It's a reminder that God forgives you and loves you. Are you ready for that?"

She looked at me, whispered something inaudible, and nodded. Holding the eye contact, I absolved her, in a nonpriestly way, because absolution is not something we do in my denomination, but it is a life-giving part of Christianity. "Barbara, God is merciful. And God is always working to reconcile with the world and with each one of us through peace and forgiveness. Know that by the grace of God, the liberating work of Christ, and the love of the Holy Spirit, your sins are forgiven."

The eye contact broke as she put her head down again and tears streamed. As she stared at the floor, we moved to some sort of subterranean emotional level, like some dormant roots were waking. And she let me know that there was more to the story.

It started when Barbara was little. She had always been a curious child, getting into every drawer and cabinet. She began to discover her body, and how good it could feel when she touched it. One afternoon, Barbara's grandmother caught her playing with herself. Horrified, her grandmother picked her up, spanked her, and called her a "filthy child." Barbara flushed with shame.

The punishment didn't stop Barbara's curiosity though. She continued and learned to hide better. As the years went on, the more pleasure she could extract, the filthier she felt. Her punishment and reward became so entwined that she couldn't extrapolate the two. Like a child who received a slap across the face before every piece of candy, she became confused about whether she ought to desire the smack. When she gave in to the man at the office, the guilt and pleasure cycle began again, and she was afraid that she didn't know how to engage a healthy sexuality.

I realized that Barbara not only sought absolution for the affair, but she needed it for her whole body. She needed some affirmation that her flesh was forgiven and good.

Our conversation reminded me of St. Augustine,

the theologian whose thought remains foundational for Christianity. Augustine opined with a bitter longing about concupiscence, or lust. He described longing lyrically, talking about his desire as it plucked at his garment of flesh. He anguished over his wet dreams and wrote copiously of their evil.[1] In Boston, members of a support group who wrestled with sex addiction found so much resonance in Augustine's *Confessions* that they named their 12-step group the Augustine Fellowship.

Not every religion had a patriarch who was a sex addict, but Christianity could claim that particular distinction. When it came to women, it was almost as if Augustine had the power to distill all of the myriad delights of our biological sex into one concoction until we became mere carnal intoxicants.

Actually, I'm not being fair. Women weren't just one thing to Augustine. The great theologian split women into two parts: *homo* and *femina*. As *homo*, women were made in the image of God. We had an intellect that could be saved. By contrast, a woman's bodily, sexual, and social nature was *femina* and represented a lower part that needed to be controlled by a man. So, a woman wasn't made in the image of God as she stood alone, but together with a husband she could be in the image of God.[2]

This thought is horrifying in so many ways—a woman does not need a man for salvation, nor should a man control a woman's sexuality. Plus, there are other, subtle movements happening here. Augustine moves the realm of sin from *what we do* to *who we are*. The sin is no longer an action, but a being, a woman. So he makes a distinct, damning move from guilt to shame when he judges not the action but the person.

The sweet truth of our faith proclaims that we are made in the image of God—female and male.[3] And in Jesus Christ there is no longer Jew or Greek, slave or free, male or female.[4]

Yet, Augustine's views on women are bitter delusions that have poisoned Christianity, relationships, and too many women. In Christianity, sexuality has often been tied to shame. For women, our bodies—as well as our actions—have been understood as shameful, even before we do anything. For Barbara, she learned that as a little girl discovering her body. For me, it was the lesson I learned on the first night as a student at Moody Bible Institute.

REVEALING HARMFUL LESSONS

On orientation night at Moody, the women went to the chapel and the men to the theater for a welcoming. Jan, the resident supervisor clicked a cassette player, the music began, and the air filled

with rhythm, followed by an electronic keyboard.
Russ Taff reached up to sing the notes above his
range,

He had no medals

and a not quite Van Halen's "Jump" riff followed. I
smiled at the woman next to me. She seemed nice.
One by one, the female resident assistants (RAs)
emerged on the stage where men ordinarily preached,
turning it into a fashion show runway.

Heroes come and heroes go

the music continued as the first RA appeared from
behind the velvety acoustic curtains and strutted
under the shining organ pipes.[5]

"This is an outfit that you could wear to class,"
Jan explained as the RA modeled something from
the GAP. She donned an oversize rugby shirt, with
blue and white horizontal stripes. Although the shirt
was big, she neatly tucked it into a long khaki skirt,
cinched with a leather belt. She looked great, but I
could never pull that off. My skirt would be all poufed
up with that added material crammed into it. The slit
in the rear did not dare to bare anything above the
back of the knee. When her calf did peek out from the
skirt, I saw that the model was wearing flesh-colored

panty hose. And on her feet, she wore shiny penny loafers that coordinated perfectly with her belt.

Every other woman pranced out in an outfit that broke the rules. The next woman was in a black skirt that hung two inches above the knee, without hosiery. Jan crossed her arms and shook her head in disdain.

I recognized the skirt, because I had one just like it.

I swallowed and tried to process how different the rules were going to be from the Florida beach town where I grew up. In Indian Harbour Beach, every restaurant had a reminder on the door: NO SHOES, NO SHIRT, NO SERVICE because the 100-degree temperature and the 100-percent humidity combo made it just that easy to walk into a dining establishment forgetting that you were wearing only a bikini top.

Now, as I watched the rule-breaking maven with her knee-revealing skirt and bright-pink shirt that divulged her cleavage, I knew I would need to make sure that neck to toe was covered. The woman coyly showed her leg as we all whooped.

"Oh, my head! Where did these girls get these clothes?" the woman next to me asked in amazement.

I started to answer that the skirt was from the Body Shop, but I stopped myself. I flushed red, avoided her eyes, and answered, "I have *no* idea."

We went through most of the clothing rules that way, until we knew what to wear and, more important, what not to wear. In class, we were to be clothed in dresses or skirts, along with appropriate hosiery. Most women seemed to wear floral patterns, with bulging roses vining a white backdrop, or Laura Ashley sweater sets. We certainly could not wear the short jean skirt with lime-green leggings that materialized on the maverick model.

The women became giddy, especially when the rebel models emerged with a tacky, shameless style. For those who had been at the school for a while, it was titillating to see the respected members of the community onstage, flaunting their oft-hidden legs. When they took the role of the immodest caricatures, lampooning the bold and the brazen, they would strut across the stage until they encountered Jan, who would shake her head and point out the unseemly thigh flesh or the wayward bra strap as everyone else tittered.

The model looked at the crowd, lifted her palms with a clueless shrug, miming, "What? I had no idea. Who knew?"

I tried to get comfortable in my chair. My lie was not sitting well with me. It was the first night, and I was already pretending to be more moral than I actually was. So, I confessed my unease to the woman next to me, "You know. I didn't actually know about *all* of these rules."

Upon hearing that, her niceness faded and she gave me an impertinent glare. "What? They sent you the

Student Life Guide when you were accepted into Moody.
Didn't you read it?"

I didn't bother to answer because it wasn't a
question. It was a scold.

I didn't remember getting the *Student Life Guide* in
the mail, but even if I had received it, it would never
have occurred to me to read it. I didn't really read
handbooks of any sort. I was a learn-as-you-go kind
of person. I started to defend myself, but I was pretty
sure that I didn't have anything that would stand
up solidly enough. Then I would have to lie again
in order to appeal to her. So I gave up on my new
acquaintance, slouched in my chair, and tried to make
friends with my developing shame.

The models displayed the wardrobe dos and don'ts
until Jan took the microphone. The music stopped
and she got serious as she further notified us that we
couldn't watch movies, except when there was a movie
night hosted by the activities council on campus. We
could not drink alcohol or dance—even if we were
the legal drinking age and at a wedding, on break,
or far away from Moody's campus. Neither could
we play "face cards," because people gambled with
those cards, so it would look bad to have students
with them. We could, however, play Rook, because
it was created specifically for Bible school students
who could not use regular cards. We could not
have televisions in our rooms, but there would be a

community TV on the second floor of the women's dorm.

We could not be alone in a room with a member of the opposite sex, and we had to refrain from all public displays of affection. If we wondered if we were sitting too close to a guy, we just had to ask ourselves, "Could a Ryrie Study Bible fit in between us?" If the answer was yes, then we were golden.

The RS explained that in order to make sure that the standards were observed, we would be denied entrance into the cafeteria unless we were dressed appropriately. "Why do we do all of this? Why do we care about what you wear?" Jan asked us, rhetorically setting up her speech. "Well, your bodies are temples of the Holy Spirit. Every one of you has your tuition paid by men and women who saved all their lives so that they could donate to Moody Bible Institute. Widows put every dime they have into your education. They invest in *you*. You can't forget the donors. These men and women come to campus and they want to see students who are preparing for God's work. They expect that you will look like ambassadors for Jesus Christ.

"You need to remember that when you get dressed every morning. As you look into the mirror, you need to say to yourself, 'I am an ambassador for Jesus Christ.'" We nodded as we assumed our mantle as the highest-ranking diplomats for the Son of God.

"But it's more than that." Jan sat down on the stage, on the front edge, so we could get more intimate with her. "The men on campus are preparing to be pastors and missionaries. Men are *different* than we are. Men become excited by sight," she said with a pinch of pity in her voice. "They have different sorts of thoughts, and what you wear triggers their imaginations. *You* can cause them to lust. *You* can make them stumble." She inhaled, closed her eyes, and held her breath for a few seconds. When she opened them they weighed us down with their solemnity. "Jesus says that if you cause your brother to stumble, 'it would be better for you if a great millstone were fastened around your neck and you were drowned in the depths of the sea.'"

With that, we were dismissed.

As the female students made it through the bottleneck exit and streamed out into the warm night, all of the pent-up energy dissipated into Chicago's starless sky. As I plodded out of the chapel, I felt my skin. I allowed my index finger to trace my neck—my throat, the back of my hairline, and then that throat again—as my head swam with the list of restrictions. I didn't think there was any way I could be good enough for Moody or for my intended profession, and I was feeling looming guilt, but I didn't know why. Other than that quick lie, I hadn't really done anything monumentally wrong since I had arrived. Then I looked down at my clothes.

I was demure compared to everyone in my hometown, but after the fashion show, I worried, *Oh God, how many men had I caused to stumble? How many millstones was I due?* On most days I didn't even feel mildly attractive. I never considered my seductive powers to be stumble-worthy.

The guilt was not about what I had done; it was about who I was. We learned at the fashion show that we needed to keep that *femina* under control. We covered it, hid it, and repressed it. *Femina*'s skirts had to be pulled down and her cleavage needed to be concealed. We understood that there was something shameful about our flesh and blood.

Not only that, but the men around us became at once predatory *and* innocent, like rabid dogs that could not help but attack. With the metaphor of "stumbling," it was as if men having sex was an involuntary action that they could not possibly be responsible for, like succumbing to gravity. It was my first lesson in Bible school, and the one I have had the most difficulty shaking throughout the ensuing years.

For many people, like Barbara and me, moving along the path of healing meant reclaiming the shards of goodness of our flesh and blood. And, like so many things we have to relearn for a more compassionate faith, I realized though toxic streams flow in the Christian tradition, there are also life-giving beliefs. There is another message we can receive from Christianity about our bodies; one of love and celebration. Alongside the damning views of the flesh within the faith, there are also traditions that understand that our skin is beautiful and God infused.

Theologians talk about this subject in terms of "incarnation" which means "in the flesh." In our mythologies, we speak of God forming us from clay and breathing life into us. In this act of creation, we are made in the image of God and we are God bearers. We understand that Jesus is God incarnate. God loved our bodies so much that Jesus was born of a woman, took on flesh and blood, and walked among us. And the belief that Jesus came back to life in bodily form indicates the importance of flesh. In communion, we break the bread, and in that act, we understand that broken flesh is holy. Throughout Christianity, we learn the goodness of the flesh.

Barbara slowly learned that goodness too. She wrote down life-giving messages from Christianity that affirmed her body and desires. She and her husband committed to rebuilding their marriage. It took years of loving and being loved, but eventually she was able to delight in her body and sex, understanding that both were a gift from God.

DRAWING UPON LESSONS IN
LOVE FROM THE CHURCH

I learned about that holy goodness through my
mom. I was a teenager, and she was on the phone
one Sunday afternoon. Her hushed voice bled with
betrayal, "I saw him in the parking lot with her. I
think he wanted to get caught." Unlike a lot of gossip,
this exchange didn't have the quality of a listener
hungry for salacious trivialities. Instead, there was
mourning in the news. The whole house felt on edge,
as I sat on the couch in an adjoining room, straining
to hear.

The bits and pieces came together. Our pastor
had an affair and confessed it in his sermon. He
stood up in front of the church and let the gathered
members know that he had succumbed to temptation,
but he was ready to just "move on." Evidently, his
sense of entitlement reached beyond his marital
commitments; it also made very awkward demands of
the congregation.

The shocked congregation was not so ready to just
"move on." They wanted details. They demanded to
know exactly what had happened, how long, and with
whom. The elders and the pastor scheduled a meeting
for that evening. As the sun went down, my father left
for the gathering of leaders.

My mother paced the kitchen a few more times. Instead of grabbing the phone again, she picked up a big basin and placed our plushest guest towels inside of it. Then she yelled out to the quiet house, "Car-ol! Let's go!"

The warm Florida night swelled with the sound of crickets singing and waves crashing as we drove for about half an hour, over a bridge, from the beach to the mainland, to our pastor's home. When we pulled up to the driveway, the house was dark. My determined mom still gathered the basin and towels and rang the doorbell. I didn't remember being let in. I just remembered entering and seeing Margaret, our pastor's wife, sitting on a chair in her living room. She remained motionless in the dark room, in her beautiful home, staring at her spotless, plush white carpet, breathing deeply.

My mother took the basin, walked into her friend's kitchen, and filled it with warm water. She carried it to Margaret's feet. Taking off Margaret's shoes, she cradled her soles as if they were the most precious things in the world. Without a word, mom put them in the water and washed them.

Margaret began to cry, and it didn't take long before the tears smeared all of our faces. Mom took Margaret's feet out and dried them on the soft towels. Throughout the entire ritual, we didn't talk much, but we know what was being said. Even as a teenager,

I understood the depth of it. Margaret was about to face some of the worst public betrayal as people began to pick apart the indiscretions of her husband.

Privately, people made extremely difficult decisions to work through a spouse's unfaithfulness every day. When it happened before an audience, the duplicity magnified. The most intimate facts of this affair would be drawn out for everyone. Margaret's character would be questioned. And people would whisper about how they would *never* put up with such a thing. Some would even wonder if Margaret was the reason. They would say she was too frigid. They would say she didn't take care of her appearance enough. They would say no wonder he had to find love elsewhere.

In the midst of the painful exposure, Margaret would sort out what she was going to do about her marriage. While hearing more details than she ever wanted to, she would have to evaluate everything in her life—her friends, the lies, her reputation, her pride, her children, and her financial situation. Mom wanted Margaret to know one thing in the midst of it: Margaret would be utterly cherished, by God and by us, even to the end of her toes.

My faith was formed that evening, not by the bitter betrayal, not by the confused congregation, but in the love of the women. Mom pulled on an ancient Christian tradition that had been practiced for thousands of years to reclaim our bodies and love for one another.

In the Bible, Mary took Jesus's feet, baptized them with her tears, and anointed him with perfume.[6] In the process, she prepared Jesus for his death, not just with the costly ointments, but with the foot-washing ritual that let him know that no matter what sort of trials he would face, he would do it realizing the love that soaked his skin.

Jesus said that whenever we spoke of the good news, we would do it in memory of her. Of course, many more Holy Week sermons focus on Judas's betrayal rather than on Mary's anointing. Mary hardly figures in when we recall the gospel.

Yet, as I walked along my path to healing, I recalled her. I remembered the reality of betrayal, but the story would always be bathed in the fragrance of her expensive perfume. I think of all the times that love had the ability to salve toxic days and allow us to face injustice and cruelty.

MAKING FRIENDS WITH MY *FEMINA*

Now, I engage in a regular discipline of honoring my body. The memory of Margaret and the story of scripture eventually allowed me to find my own healing ritual. I have a small vial of oil from Thistle

Farms, an enterprise begun in 1997 by Becca Stevens, an Episcopal priest, under the name Magdalene. The women who created the balm were part of the Magdalene community, a community for women transitioning out of sex work, trafficking, and addiction. I met the women after making a pilgrimage to Nashville and spending a morning at the factory and teahouse. We unfurled our day by lighting a candle, listening with thanksgiving as the women expressed the joys of the morning.

Looking around the room, I heard generations of gratitude. "I'm thankful for this community," a woman said while balancing her baby on her lap. "You saved my mom's life." Her mom reached over and gave her daughter a sideways hug.

Becca explained to me that most of the women started being abused when they were nine to twelve years old. Their bodies were discarded, yet they found a healing love as well as marketable skills through distilling lavender and dandelions and infusing them into the fatty liquid of olives. They took thistles and other herbs that would have been cast off and thrown away, and transformed them into something beautiful, just as they refined the splendor of their own lives. They tested the oils on their own skin and perfected the smell with their own noses.

Since that day, I joined them in their recovery, using the oil, praying for those strong women, and

trying to distill some of their resilience into my pores.
I practiced a ritual of anointing while rearranging
and repeating the compassionate messages coursing
through my tradition. I noticed as my litany became
less of a defense and more of a confession of faith.

> This is the body that has been given to me, broken as
> it is. God created this flesh and blood and declared
> that it is good—every part of it is good and made in
> the image of God. Men and women are made in the
> very image of God. *Femina* is the image of God.[7]

I closed my eyes and breathed in the knowledge.
The smell of the oil deepened my emotional
connection with the experience as the messages
entwined with the texture of my skin and the rapture
of the scent. I let the oils mingle with the memory
of all the times that I had been called filthy or a
stumbling block. I began to re-member, as the limbs
of my body became reconciled with what I believed.

My flesh was good. Abused, wounded, raped, and
beloved bodies—we were good. My hands trembled a
bit as they moved over my neck—the neck I was sure
that Jesus would noose with a millstone.

It was good.

Practicing anointing didn't come easily. I was
uncomfortable with it because of my childhood
experiences with Pentecostal fervor. When my parents

would practice anointing, they would put Crisco in
a crystal bowl, and people were often "slain in the
Spirit." Soon after a person was smeared with a bit
of oil, they passed out. Then they stood up woozy,
and the experience would have different effects on
them. Sometimes they would laugh hysterically, other
times they would move into a daze as if this world
were some kind of dream. Either way, they somehow
seemed to become separated from their bodies.

I was slain in the Spirit one time. I was about nine
when a person prayed for me and anointed my head. I
passed out, and then woke up confused and disoriented.
I was so dizzy that I could barely stand, so I crawled
into the pew next to my mom. I gripped her arm tightly
and whispered, "It's like I'm flying on a kite."

"I know! Isn't it wonderful?" She beamed.

I didn't share her enthusiasm.

This was one of the many reasons why as an adult
I got far away from those charismatic services where
the anointing oils flowed. I became Presbyterian—
stodgy and safe. I would no longer be subject to
any fainting or flying. Presbyterians remained
comfortable, worshipping God whose presence
seemed to settle us in our pews with the weight of our
big brains.

Later in seminary, when I was on a small planning
team for an Easter Vigil, my liturgy professor (the
man who taught us the art and history of leading a

worship service) suggested using oils in the service. My response perplexed everyone—even me—as I suddenly banged my head on the desk and cried, "Oh dear God, *please* tell me you're not going to get out the Crisco." My professor laughed, and the confused Presbyterians quickly removed the ritual from the service plans after my disturbing reaction.

Soon after that, within the context of a different faith tradition, anointing became a more positive practice for me. I was reminded that anointing was a ritual that went back farther than the 1970s charismatic Jesus people. It was ancient. Some people believe that it had roots with hunters and gatherers. When a man would kill an animal, he would smear the fat on his skin, in the hopes of taking on the animal's courage and strength. People used oils to select kings, celebrate unity, and pass along blessings. In our present day, we anoint people as a seal at their baptism or when we pray for healing. With this new understanding, I watched my Episcopal and Lutheran friends break out the oils on more than one occasion, while I tried not to break out in a PTSD sweat.

When no dizziness or fainting ensued, I became more comfortable. During one particular service, when a woman held my palms, rubbed oil into them, and prayed for me, something peculiar happened. I realized that this flesh was not simply a disposable outer garment. The touch became an outside

affirmation of its goodness. My flesh was not a
tarnished version of my inner self, but my flesh was *me*.

It was a completely different experience than how
I had once understood anointing, because before the
practice made me think that we should be enraptured
in some transcendental, disembodied realm. Instead,
I felt like Pinocchio becoming a real boy. I woke
up to the fact that my skin was not something to be
discarded, controlled, or hidden. It was not the origin
of evil or a stumbling block for sinners. I became aware
of my entire fleshy, spiritual humanity. With the touch,
I began to experience wholeness in a different sort of
way. Just as I longed to mend my understanding of
God, my emotions, and my metaphors, I realized that
my soul and body needed to make amends.

If I was going to heal, the act of anointing needed
to be a part of the process. I had spent a lifetime of
seeing advertisements that cheapened my body, by
saying it wasn't thin enough or that it was only good if
it was the object of the male gaze. My flesh had been
threatened and abused. I heard that it was filthy if I
enjoyed sex or if someone was attracted to it. I would
be told in a thousand different ways that my flesh
was bad. But I needed to extract a different message
and let it soak in. I began this ritual of massaging the
liquid into my skin and waking up to the wonder of
my body. As the air became heavy with the smell of
lavender, I began to look at and listen to my flesh.

Smoothing oil over my thighs, I became thankful for strong legs. Sliding my hands over my belly, I noticed the hunger and aches I might have scorned in my disordered eating. I appreciated my skin and how the years had worn it. I could see the bones and veins more clearly in my hands. I admired how scars marked significant recovery, and I imagined that the creases around my eyes increased along with crone-like wisdom. I gave thanks for the meandering curves that didn't match up with the silhouettes in any fashion magazine. I used the oil daily, spreading it over my own skin as a way to redress the issues with my past and with my flesh.

God created my flesh in God's image. It was good. It was divine.

RECLAIMING YOUR BODY

I watched a mom with her little boy. The child fell down, clearly banging his head, and the parent rushed in to say, "C'mon. Stand up. You're not bleeding. You're not hurt. Quit crying." In that moment, the boy was taught some very important lessons, namely, that (1) we should not have empathy for someone who suffers, (2) we should deny another person's pain, and (3) we do not need to listen to the pain of our own injuries.

A teen girl is hungry, but she has been told so many times that she is fat that she has a difficult time eating without feeling guilty. So she begins to ignore the ache and longings for certain food.

How do we overcome that sort of formation and learn to listen to our bodies? How do we tell the truth about our flesh? How do we trust the messages that our bodies are sending us? How do we acknowledge "I am hurting" even if our mothers say we're not? How do we understand "I am hungry" even though we live in a society that prefers emaciated women? And, when it comes to spiritual healing, how do we overcome all those damning messages that some of us heard in the church?

Think about that shattered vase again, our metaphor for a life that needs to be healed. Now, we're picking up that shard that represents the truth of our bodies, looking at it, and recovering it. As we work for spiritual healing, we need to be sure that the love of God, self, and neighbor are working together. In order to love ourselves, we will reclaim our flesh and blood goodness, and to do that we will need to listen to and appreciate our bodies.

As you begin, spend a few minutes noticing your breath and opening yourself to God. In this process, as you focus on your body, you can pray that your soul might become vulnerable and open to new wisdom.

🌹 *Unveiling False Body Messages Exercise*

Fold a piece of paper in half, lengthwise. Recall the messages that you have been told about your body.

(For example, you're "filthy" if you masturbate, "impure" if you've had sex, or a "temptation" for simply existing.) Write them down on the left side of the paper. Try to remember where you heard them. Do these messages reflect the truth of who you are in God? If not, then tell the truth on the right side. You may rely on verses like "I am wonderfully and fearfully made." "Marvelous are God's works."[8] Or affirm the truths of scripture, like "I was created in the image of God." "Male and female, God created us."

✿ *Listening to Your Body Exercise*

Begin by standing up and breathing deeply. Roll your head, very gently, three times clockwise and three times counterclockwise. Shake out your arms, your legs, your middle, and your voice. Hug yourself. Bend over, then slowly stand up. Think about how your feet connect to the ground. Rub your hands together to create heat, mush your face, and massage your scalp. Walk a little bit. In this way, you can become fully present in your body and your surroundings.[9]

Stop and breathe. What is your body saying? Are you hungry for certain foods? Do you have other cravings? Do you have pain to which you need to attend? What parts of your body feel good? What do you appreciate about your body?

🌺 *Anointing Exercise*

If you would like to establish an anointing ritual with a group, you can get some oil (Thistle Farms oils are available online, at thistlefarms.org) and pray:

> Praise God who made heaven and earth. Your word brought light out of darkness. You molded us from the dust of the earth and blew life into us. Your spirit renews the earth. We praise you because Jesus Christ, the anointed one, brought healing to those in weakness and distress. By the power of your spirit, may you bless those who are anointed with this oil. May they be made whole, restored in your spirit and renewed in your love.

Then, you can put oil on a finger or a thumb, saying:

> May Christ bring you wholeness,
> In mind, in body, and in spirit.
> May the peace of Christ be with you.

Make the sign of the cross on a person's forehead or hand, saying,

> (Name), I anoint you in the name of God, who gives you life. Receive the healing, forgiveness,

and love of Christ. And in the Spirit of God, be at peace.[10]

You can also adapt the prayer, if you would like to practice the ritual alone.

✸ *Practicing Gratitude Exercise*

Many of us grew up giving thanks to God before our food. It might have become a mindless ritual or an embarrassing display of piety. Try to embrace the ritual again (you can do it silently), not as a way to let everyone in a restaurant know how religious you are, or as a means of converting people, but as a practice of gratitude. As you eat, mindfully chew, tasting your food, and delighting in the wonder of the act.

If you're able to go on walks, spend the first few minutes constructing a list of things for which you are thankful. Start with the air you breathe and the ground beneath your feet. If you have healthy parts of your body, name them. With each step, name something that makes you grateful. By connecting what you're thankful for and your steps, you will begin to have an embodied practice of gratitude.

Chapter 7

REGAINING OUR HOPE

Shawna, a member of our church, came into my office wearing her workout clothes. She had just been to the gym, the place where she was able to think. Pulling a paperback from her bag, she placed it on my desk. I knew what it was before my eyes could focus on the letters, because the black book with its flaming band had been ubiquitous in bookstores, retail stores, and even some grocery stores—*Left Behind* by Tim LaHaye and Jerry B. Jenkins.

"Do you think it could happen this way?" Shawna asked.

"No," I said, and watched her tense shoulders immediately relax. The fear fell off of her, like a vestigial tail disappearing in the evolutionary process.

"I know. I know. It's ridiculous," then she double-checked. "Are you *sure* it won't happen this way?"

"Yes. I'm sure," I gave her my most confident minister face in the hopes it would soothe her, and continued. "You know how each week we pray, 'your kingdom come, your will be done, on earth as it is in heaven'?"

Shawna nodded.

"*That's* what we believe. We pray that because we have a hopeful view for all of creation."

I picked up the book and smiled.

I met Jenkins before his books took up multiple shelves at the used bookstore and inspired Nicolas Cage to play the starring role of the film adaptation. Jerry Jenkins worked as the author-in-residence at Moody. My mother and I visited his office during one of my first days on campus.

Moody's theology must have percolated in Jenkins's imagination, for on campus students had an uncanny excitement that Jesus would return. Jesus would descend from the clouds and gather the true believers in a physical Rapture. Any geopolitical event became an alarm warning that Jesus was coming again. Any unrest in the Middle East cued the approaching Armageddon. Any charismatic figure with opposing political views was probably the Antichrist. Any natural disaster would be greeted with, "See? I told you so. Jesus is on his way." The fact that Israel had become a nation was undeniable proof that the red carpet had been rolled out for Christ's arrival. Signs of the times flashed around us like neon on the Vegas Strip.

We talked about the end of the world constantly. In fact, friends even played practical jokes on classmates by leaving out clothes in the hallway and hiding to make it look like the Rapture had occurred.

We joked about the Rapture, not because we thought it was absurd. It was real and scary. It seems strange to me now, but for the first couple decades of my life, I worried about how and when Jesus would come back and dreaded this horrifying event until the thought of it seemed to leave a toxic, powdery anthrax coating on my plans. It was almost as if someone had stolen my future from me.

When I was growing up, preachers showed us how to do Rapture exercises. Starting with deep knee bends, they outstretched their arms, and scissored into a Superman jump. At Moody, professors—gray-headed white men who wore tweed suits and wrote Ph.D. after their names—elucidated how we would ascend into heaven in almost every introductory course.

I sat through the familiar lecture in Dr. Root's course. He strolled about the room, with a Bible in one hand and bifocals in the other. He drew a large line on the chalkboard and situated a cross on the plane, about three-quarters from its beginning. Then Root began to section off the line into seven other distinct parts.

"In different times, God relates to man in different

ways," Root explained. "And we understand these eras as dispensations." We copied down the dispensations, organizing the complex, chaotic narrative of the Bible into a neat and tidy time line—something that readily fit on a chalkboard.

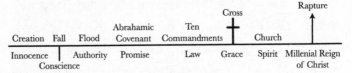

The dispensation of God's grace answered the question, "What must a person do to be saved?" Salvation, in our classroom, primarily focused on what it would take for a person to go to heaven. Since our conservative tradition answered that question in one way, while the Bible described salvation in a multitude of ways, dispensationalism divided our relationship with God into various eras. Each dispensation ended with humanity's failure, and so God had to start relating to us some other way.

Root explained each era to us. The Creation was a time of innocence. But when Eve enticed Adam to consume the fruit from the tree of knowledge of good and evil, the Fall occurred, allowing sin to taint our human existence. With their new understanding and loss of innocence, God could no longer relate to humanity in the same way, and the means of grace changed.

After the Fall, people relied on their conscience

to understand the difference between right and wrong, good and evil. The human conscience proved unreliable. Humanity became so corrupt that God charged Noah to build a boat, and then God sent a Flood. During that time of destruction and rebuilding, humanity was under an era of God's authority. That means of grace changed and humanity entered a different era with the Covenant that God made with Abraham.

Then, God introduced the Law. Through Moses, God presented the Ten Commandments, and obeying the Law became the way to earn God's grace. Unfortunately, since no one could fully live up to all the mandates, we failed again.

So Jesus came, his death was the sacrifice that ended the dispensation of the Law and we moved into an age of grace. The Church age started at Pentecost. According to Root, humanity was obviously failing this round as well, so we await the next dispensation—the second coming of Jesus—which would feature the Rapture.

Based on the promises God made with a half dozen men—Adam, Noah, Abraham, Moses, Jesus (who was also God), and Paul—the past made perfect sense. Predicting the future proved to be more challenging, and the mystery made it frightening. With the Rapture, Jesus would descend from the heavens, and people would ascend to meet him in the sky. Some would be left behind, as chaos ensued. The sun would turn to blood, there would be wars, there would be no bread, and all sorts of desolation would take place. It was all terrifying.

The events certainly were not clearly foretold in the Bible. When I studied the book of Revelation, the letter came off more as an acid trip than a guide to the future. John's visions seemed more mystical than factual predictions.

I admired the security of my classmates; they knew they would be the victors, but my ultimate salvation didn't feel so certain for me. I figured I would do something to lose my ticket to heaven. When people predicted the rapturous events, I rarely imagined myself on the winning side.

I wondered what this narrative was doing to us Bible school students. I supposed that if Jesus was the savior of American Christianity, we needed an ending more Hollywood than baffled disciples staring up at Jesus's ankles. So we imagined that Jesus, our cosmic big brother, would return triumphantly to settle the score. Yes, it was humiliating to evangelize people in the airport and go through all sorts of embarrassing situations, but in the end, vengeance was God's. And as long as I could figure out how to remain on God's side, vengeance would also be mine.

Yet, what did it mean for us to live our lives, expecting an unhappy ending? How did it affect us to anticipate separation from our loved ones and the destruction of the earth? What did this story do to our spirits? Did it stoke a victimhood and vengeance among us? I looked around at my classmates, as the lecture ended and they filed out of the room. Even with all the destruction, I don't think it was a bad ending, in their minds. But I began to have dispensational doubts.

Years later, as I served as a pastor and Shawna stood in my office, I heard how the idea of the Rapture frightened her as well. She had been told so many times that humanity was going to hell and that the truly faithful would be raptured that when she was a child and she would find herself suddenly alone, the first thing she would imagine was that she had been "left behind."

She recalled one afternoon in particular, when she was blow-drying her hair and belting out an Amy Grant song into her hairbrush. When she shut off the hair dryer and stopped singing, her house seemed ominously quiet. She listened for her family, and when she could not hear them, she became horrified that the Rapture occurred and she had not only been abandoned by God, but that God had also taken her family away from her and left her orphaned.

With desperation, she searched the house, finding no one. Her panic heightened when she went outside. Eventually, she found her mom and dad out near the shed. They all laughed when they were reunited, but decades later that shattering sense of abandonment stuck with Shawna. As Shawna raised her own daughters, she wanted a more life-giving idea of God and the future than the one she had been taught.

I agreed. "What's the point of religion if it doesn't give us hope?" I wondered. "We don't need all of that destruction to be satisfied, do we? If we don't need it, I'm sure God doesn't need it." We began to focus on the prayer that Jesus taught us. What did it say about the future? "Your kingdom come, your will be done, on earth as it is in heaven." Surely, it was not just a prayer but also a commission. It was a daring to dream and work for a world that might be like heaven.

SHIFTING FROM INDIVIDUAL SALVATION TO UNIVERSAL LIBERATION

I continued to dismantle my faithful ideas of the future when I was at Moody. At that time, Moody was situated between Cabrini-Green and the Gold Coast, which meant our school was the base of an unbalanced seesaw, with one of the most violent housing projects on one end and one of the most opulent neighborhoods on the other end. I spent my weeks working with kids in the projects one day and babysitting for elite families the next. Before then, I always assumed that everyone in the United States had a level playing field, and that if children worked hard enough, they would be rewarded in adulthood with a comfortable life. But moving from Cabrini to the Gold Coast shattered my middle-class myths. I realized that a child's entire future could almost be scripted, depending on which block he or she resided.

As I sorted out the end-times and the inequities, I didn't imagine that the two had much to do with one another until I picked up Walter Rauschenbusch's *Christianity and the Social Crisis.* Rauschenbusch had been a pastor in Hell's Kitchen in New York City. The neighborhood's graphic name fit better at the turn of the twentieth century, when small children worked in factories and laborers were expected to put in grueling and protracted hours. Rauschenbusch became sick from praying over tiny coffins, and he called upon the church to think about salvation beyond individualistic terms. His passionate preacher's rhetoric echoed through the centuries, from Hell's Kitchen to Cabrini-Green as he described the kingdom of God as the "world as it ought to be."

I always imagined that "being saved" meant that I would go to heaven. It was a personal thing. I stood for an altar call at a Michael W. Smith concert and invited Jesus into my heart. Salvation promised heaven, but in this life it didn't go farther than being an individual admonishment to be a good girl—to not go "too far" when I was out on a date and to keep my red Dixie cup filled with Diet Coke rather than the golden nectar flowing from the keg. As if the beautiful sweeping movement of God's work of creation, God's longing for unity and reconciliation, was solely distilled in my solitary angst over celibacy and soberness.

Reading the words of Rauschenbusch, understanding what my faith had to do with the injustices that surrounded me, ignited a greater hope. "Salvation" shifted for me. It was not an individual entry ticket into the pearly gates that I earned by being good; it was a way of abundant life. It was a struggle to love my neighbor as I loved myself. It was not just a personal experience of being saved from my sin. It was also an understanding of the greater context of God's work among systemic wrongs.

It was as if I had been focusing on the beauty of a single piece of yarn for years, and suddenly I realized that little piece of fiber was part of a moving, living tapestry of vibrant color and motion. I had been content with the prosperity gospel, baptizing the inequities as God's will, but I was realizing that what I did affected others. What they did affected me. And in this alternative vision, I could believe that God longed for us all to have abundant lives.

I not only understood salvation differently, but I

also began to understand the end-times differently. This longing continued for years as I worked as a minister with people in poverty in different settings. I deepened my understanding of the liberation of God, the saving work of God for the orphan, widow, prisoner, and powerless. I could no longer pray "here on earth as it is in heaven" while not caring if people were hungry or homeless.

As Abraham Maslow taught us, a healthy person has a hierarchy of needs—physiological, security, and social needs—that he displayed on a pyramid.[1] Feeling fed, safe, and loved are important for a person's development. In contrast, the end-time fantasies Shawna and I were taught as children wounded us when they predicted famine, war, blight, and abandonment. They threatened our physiological needs. When we talked about the Rapture all the time, we lived our lives on bleeding-red high alert, without a sense of safety. The idea that God was willing to torture humanity, leave children orphaned, and cause destruction so that Christ might return to reign threatened that pyramid.

This end-times view could also lead to a fatalism when it came to basic inequities. I not only expected my needs to be threatened, but if people were not white Evangelicals, then their devastation was part of God's plan. As our sense of security was endangered, we neglected the needs of others. Why work on changing the world when it was going to be destroyed soon anyways? God was simply stacking the decks for end-time events. It was as if Maslow's hierarchy of needs pyramid was being dismantled one layer at a time, insuring psychological discord for myself and the acceptance of scarcity for others. I couldn't love my neighbor as I loved myself.

Healing came when I longed to reconstruct the bottom of that pyramid, not only for myself, but for others. When I began to read Rauschenbusch, I could no longer think of the future as the vengeance and destruction of an angry God but rather as a yearning for renewal and liberation. I imagined the end-time not as a dread but as a dream. The world doomed became the "world as it ought to be." Reconstructing the pyramid meant looking at physical and spiritual needs, then working and protesting for that world. Salvation was not a personal act between Jesus and white Evangelical me. Instead, it was a hope, a longing, and a dream for all of us.

Shawna also worked on deconstructing her Rapture fears in much the same way I did. She read a lot of theology and now she not only teaches her children more life-giving ways of thinking about the future but also teaches them to her church.

LEARNING THE LITURGIES
OF LONGING

For years, I read all of this theology and wrestled with
it intellectually, but it took me much longer to actually
embody it. That didn't happen until one Advent, the
season we infuse our liturgies with the prayer, "Come,
Lord Jesus!"

When I was still in my twenties, I was serving my
first parish, in South Louisiana. The denomination
considered our congregation a "maintenance church."
Basically, they were waiting until the doors closed. In
front of the Communion table, I felt like a very young
woman. I was short. I swam in my preaching robe
and the tassels on the end of my stole dragged on the
ground.

The area was stringently Roman Catholic. When
I wore my clergy collar, people looked at me with
visceral disgust. I once heard someone say, "Look at
her. She thinks she's a priest."

So I struggled, yet somehow the tiny church grew.
People began to join the congregation. For the first
time in decades, the service filled with the sounds of
children singing, talking, and disrupting my sermon.
It was wonderful.

After a couple of years, I became pregnant and was
terrified to tell the congregation. I, personally, had

never seen a pregnant pastor. I had only read about
one in a John Irving novel. There was a Canadian
minister who was pregnant a lot, and for some strange
reason that very minor character gave me comfort.
At least until I began to identify another, very major
character.

We turned to Mary's story during Advent. She was
a poor young woman who found herself pregnant.
A messenger came and told her that she would bear
the son of God. Mary responded, "Let it be done
according to your word."

Meister Eckhart, a medieval philosopher and
mystic, saw this as a crucial moment. Eckhart
wrote that we flow out of God our Creator. God
was perpetually creating us; we were living in the
mind of God and always being stretched and formed
and molded. At this point in time, Mary, in her
determination, first gives spiritual birth to God, and
now God is eternally borne. Every good soul that
longs for God bears God and gives birth to God.[2]

I thought about Eckhart's words as the months went
on and my stomach stretched. Then, I experienced a
moment that forever changed my view of myself as a
Christian and of God and salvation. I was in my third
trimester, repeating the ancient Words of Institution,
when my belly began shifting around with those
smooth oceanic movements. I looked down and even
under that giant black robe, I could see it moving,

transforming into those alien shapes. My baby was just waking up and stretching. I smiled and thought, *Oh no. Not now. Please, go back to sleep!*

I continued to look down, but this time, my eyes searched for the lines in my prayer book, and I began reading the liturgy. I was afraid that I would become so distracted that I would lose my place if I said the words from memory, and so I lifted up the cup and resumed,

> This cup is the new covenant sealed in my blood, shed for you for the forgiveness of sins.
> Whenever you drink it,
> do this in remembrance of me.

It was no longer a gentle rolling. I felt jabs, right under my rib cage. As I held the cup up, I gasped as she began to play soccer with my internal organs. My eyes widened and I almost spilled the wine as she kicked me, hard. And I could barely contain my laughter as I continued:

> Every time you eat this bread and drink this cup,
> You proclaim the saving death of our risen Lord,
> until he comes.[3]

I stood there breathing deeply while this great and wonderful pain stretched me and transformed me, and with each jolt, a tremendous sense of creative power flooded me as I prayed, "Come, Lord Jesus, come!"

Suddenly, this thought of Jesus coming again, which always filled me with such anxiety and fear, gave me hope. In that moment, as I spoke of Advent dreams—my belly stretched as I broke the bread and poured the wine, I was filled with joy and longing instead of fear or vengeance. The yearning was deeper than what I'd felt growing up as a child and waiting for Christmas, because it encompassed the pain and sorrows as well as the anticipation, like moving from the taste of a cloying soda to the complex bitterness and sweetness of a fine wine.

The deep yearning was emotional, but it was physical too. As a pregnant host at that table, hope came alive in my very marrow as I felt a full-bodied longing. My muscles and bones adjusted in anticipation for the new life that was to come.

I felt at home for the first time in my body *and* behind that table, as I also understood the longing for Christ to be among us. I understood that it was a hope for the world as it ought to be—one that lifted the lowly and filled the hungry.[4] I knew that just as I longed to provide for the child forming inside of me, God longed to provide for me.

Jesus wasn't going to arrive on a mushroom cloud, with a double-edged sword coming out of his mouth

in a kick-ass move of final vengeance. Christ would
not appear to bring death and destruction.

Christ returned here and there, in our hope and
work to make things on earth as they were in heaven.[5]
Christ appeared in our caring for the earth and
for one another as we broke bread and drank wine
together. Christ came in new life and fecundity. He
came again as we served the world, striving to make
the earth into the dream of God.

As I delivered the bread and the wine to the
congregation, I remembered Mary and those
mysterious words of Eckhart. I was blessed. I was
pregnant with hope and bursting with new life. And I
was bearing God.

IMAGINING OUR HOPES

The Hebrew Bible is full of stories of how God
brought manna and daily bread. The promises of
Jesus ring true: God will supply our needs. Look at
the lilies of the field. God clothes them beautifully.[6]
Throughout our text, we understand that it is God's
hope that all might be sheltered, nourished, and
loved. Many of us, however, were raised with another
message of the Rapture and end-times destruction
that made us fear abandonment and judgment either
for ourselves or for others. These notions of our

future broke that simple machine of love (the concept that love of God, self, and neighbor work together), because the Rapture portrayed God as vengeful and our neighbors as deserving destruction.

Our goal of healing in this area is to restore a sense of justice and hope to replace those messages of vengeance and devastation. To do that, we need to imagine our own hopes, understand latent fears, and take steps to work for the dream of God. We can begin by breathing deeply and opening ourselves to God.

✿ *Finding Hope Exercise*

In this exercise, we will go back to the idea that God loves all of humanity and creation and construct a hope and dream based on that love. What would that look like?

Get out a sheet of paper or your journal and write on the top: "The world as it ought to be." Then number the lines beneath, one through twenty-five. Fill in the numbers with descriptions of your vision of what you hope for the world. Don't think much about them, but write whatever comes to mind.

Look over your list. If you're studying this with a group, then you can talk about your answers. What sort of commonalities do the words have? Do your dreams describe a way people relate to one another?

Do your hopes include all people? If not, can you rewrite them so that they do? Do your faithful hopes for the world match your politics? Is there something you left out? Then add it.

Distill your list. Write down the hopes and dreams that you have for the world in a few sentences. They might look like the following:

- We would live at peace with one another.

- We would dismantle our weapons.

- We would learn to care for creation.

If you're more of a visual person, feel free to draw at any time during this exercise. Now, if you have those dreams for the world, wouldn't God's hope be even greater and more beautiful?

Spend a few moments in silence. You can resume your open posture (sitting, with feet on the floor and palms up in your lap). Meditate on the words "on earth as it is in heaven."

❧ *Revealing Your Fears*

Did you grow up in a faith tradition that threatened your safety and security? Write down or tell a story about when you felt afraid because of a religious belief. Was there a time when a sermon scared you?

Did you have an experience when you thought you had been abandoned? Were you ever manipulated into making a religious decision because of a threat?

As you look over that story, be gentle with yourself for believing what you were told. Remind yourself that God loves you and God is for you.

🌺 *Stopping the Fear Exercise*

Imagine a child whom you love. Cast him or her in your role in your story. Now change the story so that it reflects love and hope for that child.

If you were terrorized by a sermon, what sort of sermon would you preach? If you were afraid that you had been abandoned, what would you say to that child when you reunited with him or her? What sort of truths would you want to impart to a child whom you love? If you were manipulated into a religious decision because of a threat (you would go to hell, the end-times would be devastating, or you would be cut off from your family), then think of the life-giving messages you would tell a child (you will never be separated from the love of God, and your family will love you no matter what sort of religious decisions you make).[7]

Now, realize that God loves you even more than you love that child. Reclaim those loving sermons, words, and messages for yourself.

❧ *Imagining the World as It Ought to Be*

Look over your hopes again. Think about the people with whom you come in contact. What would the "world as it ought to be" look like for them? Are there things that feel out of alignment in your neighborhood? Is there racism, domestic violence, or environmental abuse? Is there something that you have always wanted to advocate for and never found the time? Could this be the time to begin working on earth as it is in heaven? Commit yourself to one thing.

Chapter 8

REASSESSING OUR FINANCES

"I don't think I'll ever forgive myself for having to declare bankruptcy. It's been five years, and I haven't come close," Renita confessed before she even uttered hello.

I sipped a cup of coffee and balanced my cookie on a flimsy plate while trying to catch up with Renita's train of thought. A jarring thing about being a minister is that sermons set up a one-sided intimacy. It's akin to being an author, in as much as when people feel a connection to the writer before she has a chance to get to know them. I was the guest preacher at a conference, and I had just talked about forgiveness and finances when Renita cornered me during a break. The buzz and hum in the hotel conference room afforded us enough privacy in order to build that bond both ways.

Renita told me how her father and mother
were both successful, as an architect and a lawyer,
respectively. They expected great things from Renita,
so they sent her to expensive private schools. When
Renita graduated, she dreamed of starting her own
company, and she did. It all went well until her main
client went out of business. After losing his contract,
she spent months staying optimistic, trying to work
it all out. She covered her personnel expenses with
other accounts and focused on building a larger
client base. She negotiated cheaper rental agreements
and borrowed money, but she still had to lay off two
employees. The business kept bleeding, so she got a
second mortgage on her house to cover other costs.

Renita's anxiety grew as she hid bills from her
husband and tried to keep up appearances with her
colleagues. Quietly, she met with a lawyer to find
out what her options were. The lawyer suggested
bankruptcy, but she held strong. She considered
bankruptcy to be a moral failing.

Finally, Renita developed health issues with all the
strain. When her husband found out the extent of
their financial distress and her attempts to hide it from
him, their marriage almost dissolved. When she had
no other choice, she filed.

When Renita tried to explain the bankruptcy to
her mom, her mother never offered any support. She
only shook her head bitterly and muttered, "We put

so much into you. I can't believe we *wasted* so much on you."

Even though Renita's mother should have loved and supported her daughter through the financial difficulties in the same way that she would have stood by her through a surgery or a house fire, Renita's value had diminished in her mother's eyes. In all of this, Renita didn't just feel rejected by her mother, but also by God.

As soon as Renita explained what happened, I felt empathetic pains and nodded my head. "I'm sorry," I said. "Your mom has a transactional view of relationships. It's very common in our culture."

Renita's mother viewed her daughter as a commodity into which she invested. That's how she showed her parental love. Renita, in return, was to make good on the investment. That was how she was to prove her love as a daughter and her worth as a person. Then Renita took this idea of love and reflected it in her relationship with God. She expected that if she worked hard, God would provide financial security. In return, she thought that God's love for her depended on her asset balance. When the money ran out, so did her sense of being loved.

She had been working for years to build up her bank balance, but in order to forgive herself, she had some spiritual healing to do as well.

UNDERSTANDING TRANSACTIONAL RELATIONSHIPS

I couldn't always identify this twisted exchange for love, until I sat in the therapist's chair, tracing the baby-blue brocade and trying to make sense of my history with money. It was Christmastime and I had been at the mall. My daughter asked for something, and I answered, "No. I'm sorry. We don't have any money."

For her, that was the end of it. But not for me.

A few minutes later, I found myself silently praying, *O God, forgive me. Forgive me. Please, please forgive me.* I caressed the soft chenille of a pair of J. Crew socks as I uttered the plea. Then I stopped, looked down at my hand, surprised at the lump forming in my stomach. We didn't have any money and my daughter didn't need the item. Why was I feeling so anxious?

In addition to that strange shame over not being able to buy my daughter something she wanted, I felt dread about the gifts I received. It was odd because I was a frugal person and I wasn't usually materialistic. My life was full. Our house was full. I didn't need anything. But then Christmas Day would arrive and all sorts of longings would show up with it. We would travel to see our extended family, and I became envious of other people's gifts, comparing them to what I received. Then I became angry with myself.

"What is going on?" I asked the counselor, who had a sophisticated understanding of family systems.

"Carol, we all require love. Since you grew up with a volatile father, you received confusing emotional responses when you yearned for that love. But people are resilient and we learn to get what we need. You are resilient, so you began to look for love in other ways. Gifts are tangible. They have a price. You can measure them. Your father was good at giving them. So gifts became a sign of your worth and the proof of your parents' affection."

I had developed a transactional view of relationships. With that simple explanation, my therapist gave me the key that unlocked a whole hallway of mysterious doors in my mind. As a parent, I felt guilty about not being able to give my daughter something that she wanted because I feared I couldn't properly love her. As a family member, I was weighing my gifts as if they were measures of how much people loved me.

The key also unlocked a truth that went beyond parental love and had a deeper spiritual significance, because I recognized that I looked at God's favor in the same way. I had done some work and realized that salvation was larger than my individual struggles, but on a gut level, I couldn't shake the idea that God's love corresponded to the digits on my checking account.

Like a lot of middle-class Americans, I did
everything I was supposed to. Juggling multiple
jobs, I worked my way through college and graduate
school. My husband and I took opportunities in
tandem, trying to build our careers. Yet, our finances
reflected the same reality as many other families who
are my age or younger. Housing prices had gone up,
medical costs had risen, and education expenses had
skyrocketed, while salaries remained stagnant. People
went deeper into debt for everyday living. During
many points of our life, the numbers didn't add up.
Even with two professional jobs, we would be much
worse off than my parents. When I couldn't figure
out how to pay the mortgage, I felt like God had
abandoned me. Or I felt ashamed, as if I had done
something wrong and my financial struggles were
immoral. I didn't feel like I had value or worth. So I
breathed my plea for forgiveness as I felt the chenille
that was far out of my reach.

LEARNING FROM HISTORIC UPHEAVAL

Why do people so often equate money and love? Why
did I seek God's blessing in my financial security or
see divine disapproval in the lack thereof? I could see
the thinking forming with Moody's history.

Moody Bible Institute had fascinating beginnings, springing up from the streets of downtown Chicago in 1886. I imagined what it must have been like, with the air thick with foul odors wafting from the slaughterhouses and rising up from the horse manure caked in the cracks between the brick paving. The avenues teemed with people looking for work.

Men arrived from all over the country and the world to find jobs. The Industrial Revolution was well under way in Chicago, creating factories and employment as well as deplorable working conditions, a devastating economic depression, and gaping financial disparities. In the late nineteenth century, the term "robber baron" became an apt descriptor of men who amassed great wealth by squandering national resources and paying minuscule wages. Immigrants flooded into Chicago with the hope of jobs, but much of the labor was short term or seasonal, so they often found unemployment instead.

Grumblings for radical change rose up where disparities festered most. Months before the Moody Bible Institute was established, Anarchists and Communists called out from the Haymarket Riot for workers' rights. Laborers demanded an eight-hour workday and protested the police brutality that was being used during the unrest.

Many people of faith rose up, crying out for solidarity and workers' rights. Ministers spoke for a full hour during the Haymarket Riot. The Social Gospel started in New York City, and Walter Rauschenbusch's message soon spread as people all over the country began to imagine a "world as it ought to be" and stand against the economic disparities. The Woman's Christian Temperance Union encouraged women to "do everything," especially speak in public, own businesses, and engage in social issues.

Organizations born in the midst of such upheaval typically served either to midwife change or to conserve the existing structures. While Dwight L. Moody, the revivalist, preached for utter transformation at a personal level, when his message became institutionalized, it became a stronghold of conservatism holding fast against the progressive developments of the day.

Moody the man defied the threats of socialism, communism, and anarchism by personifying the possibility of an individual's movement from poverty to prosperity in a capitalist system. The preacher's own rags-to-riches story inspired so many young men at his YMCA class, that they took "before" and "after" pictures, depicting boys as grubby street urchins before attending D. L.'s lessons and scrubbed-up professionals after being under his influence. Moody billed himself as a businessman, acquired the financial backing of moguls like Cyrus

McCormick, and flanked himself with successful men
at his revivals.[1] Furthermore, Moody held segregated
revivals.[2] Moody's actions upheld individual salvation
in the religious and economic spheres, which created
strong resistance against the community, solidarity,
and organization that workers, women, and African
Americans needed.

I don't know what D. L. Moody would think about
capitalism now. People still protest for higher wages
and against police brutality, echoing the Haymarket
Riot, but today's billionaires seem more removed from
the streets and mute to the cries.

Our economy has different features than it used
to, partly brought about by the introduction of debt
without relationship. A hundred years ago, a person
might have received a loan from a local bank. The
banker would have known the kind of person he was
lending to, whether he could repay the loan, and what
hardships might be going on in his life. Now banks
are multinational conglomerates and a borrower
struggles to get anyone on the phone to talk about a
payment plan. Banks cut up mortgages, like pieces of
a pie, and sell them to other financial institutions, so
that someone who owes money on a house may have
no idea whom they actually owe.

Religion responded to our nation's financial
disparities by picking up Moody's mantle. Many
churches enmeshed capitalism and religion through

the beliefs of the prosperity gospel, until the prosperity gospel became much louder than the Social Gospel.

The prosperity gospel imagines faith as palpably demonstrated by wealth and places the individual over community.[3] Its message that "God wants to bless you with wealth" pulsed through radios, television, and megachurches, disseminating the idea that money equals the good life, and that if you do what the Lord wants, then you will reap those blessings. There are different shades of prosperity gospel, of course. The spectrum extends from slick televangelist telling us that God would take him home if his followers didn't open up their wallets, to smug religious Right pundits saying that we need to pull ourselves up by our bootstraps when we endure a medical crisis that puts us in debt for tens of thousands of dollars. The shadow side of these beliefs can heap shame on the poor and lead to the understanding that those who struggle deserve their lot in life.

While many religious voices celebrated prosperous living, our individual debt increased and became normalized so much that young adults who attend college incur student loans before they have any chance of a job interview. As the years go on, the debt continues to mount with a house and car. As a nation, we work more and more hours, but we can hardly pay off the interest. Most Americans even go into retirement with debt, but we don't talk about it much, because of that moral shame surrounding what we owe. As we keep hiding our hardships, individual responsibility turns into isolated suffering.

Prosperity gospel lifts up money as if it will make our lives abundant. It calls American greed good, the pursuit of the individual holy, and the pillaging of the earth sacred. It baptizes a transactional relationship with God, so that we begin to understand ourselves as consumers in a profound, theological sense. And so we consume—our land, our resources, and even one another—until the warning in the Letter to Galatians becomes all too real: "If, however, you bite and devour one another, take care that you are not consumed by one another."

The system in which we are trapped isn't just financial. It's spiritual. Each week, people like Renita go to church and the pews sag with the weight of stress, anxiety, and depression from economic issues, but they are afraid to say anything out loud about it. With debt, young couples put off getting married; they can't buy a house or set down roots in their communities. For those who are married, the stress and shame around finances can create marital discord. While gathering community can resolve many financial struggles, economic insecurity can cut us off from our neighbors so that we lose sight of how to measure our real worth, as loving and beloved people.

BIBLICAL ACCOUNTS

There is resonance with our current condition and
the biblical narrative. In the Hebrew Bible, the Jewish
people were also in debt. The Egyptian rulers had set
up stores of food, so that when a famine hit the land,
all of the people surrounding them had to borrow
from them in order to survive. Even though it was
one of Abraham and Sarah's descendants who had
encouraged the pharaoh to set up the stores of grain
in the first place, as the years went by, the gratitude
for that act was quickly forgotten, and the Jewish
people became entrenched as debt slaves to the
pharaoh.

As we tell this story in Sunday school and sermons,
we know that the Egyptians were the oppressors and
the Israelites fled for their freedom. God liberated
the people of Israel by sending plagues and drowning
the pharaoh's soldiers. But somehow a crucial aspect
of the story gets lost in translation. In our current
situation, we imagine the debtors as sinful.

The concepts of lending and borrowing are clear in
the Bible: We cannot serve God and money. Money
becomes idolized when we imagine that it is the key to
the good life or when we allow it to break the bonds
of community. And we should lend to those who need
it, without interest and with the full realization that
the borrower may never pay us back. Inherent in

these stipulations is the realization that lending and borrowing should be done within relationship, and the bonds of community should be stronger than the love of money.[4]

Of course, this seems like an illusory dream, as we have grown so far away from it. Now, we shame the debtors rather than those who lend with interest, even if that interest is 24 percent.

I was not the only one who confused personal finances with God's favor. A friend of mine, Bec Cranford, grew up with prosperity-gospel thinking in a Pentecostal denomination. She went into debt for seminary. Then when she changed her views regarding same-sex relationships and started speaking out for LGBTQ rights, she could no longer stay in her denomination. Suddenly, she found herself with student loan debt and no way to find a position in her intended profession. So Bec began a church and got a job waiting tables. Sometimes she would work for eight hours and come home with only thirty dollars in tips.

On one of those evenings, she became overwhelmed and locked herself in the restaurant bathroom to cry. Through her tears, she heard God. She got up and started driving around Atlanta, looking at the sex workers and those experiencing homelessness. Then she clearly heard a voice saying, "This is who you are to love." Since that day, Bec has worked with those who sleep outside. Through her vulnerability, she learned to see others in need and she was able to build relationships and community in the midst of their common humanity.

I have watched Bec and others overcome the isolation of debt. They find solidarity by courageously telling their stories, seeking common ground, and affirming God's love in the midst of it all. Growing in beloved community means that we turn away from the lie that we can flourish independently and turn toward one another and God in absolute dependence.

Hearing stories like Renita's and Bec's often leads me to the existential theologian Friedrich Schleiermacher. Schleiermacher wrote about religion as a feeling of absolute dependence. This feeling of dependence is our God consciousness; it connects us with the infinite. It is a profound chasm that we're always trying to fill with more work, entertainment, stuff, or distraction. We think that it can be filled with titles or success. But at the end of the day, it's still there, because the feeling is a longing for the existence of God.[5]

When bill collectors call, we lose our job, we get a divorce, or we suffer through grief, then we cannot be distracted from that hole. We feel it—the failure, disappointment, and loneliness. We become aware of that chasm, gaping so wide that we cannot help but fall into it. With Schleiermacher, that feeling moves us into a deeper communion with the Holy One. Dependence is absolute, and when we sense it, it siphons us to God.

Schleiermacher upholds dependence rather than autonomy, which is what Bec taught me on this journey. While prosperity can move us further into isolation, sharing our suffering helps us to overcome shame, build solidarity, and negotiate community. In all of it, we can become more aware of those precious feelings of dependence and the existence of God in our lives.

SHEDDING THE IDOL OF MONEY

Many of us get caught up in a transactional view of relationships. We feel loved according to how successful or moneyed we are. Not only that, but we can also start believing that God shows love through health and wealth. When we believe these things, what happens when we face financial difficulties beyond our control? When we lose a job, suffer a health issue, get a divorce, or find ourselves in debt, we can feel anxious from financial stress as well as abandoned by God.

To heal from the wounds in the realm of our finances, we will need to unravel ourselves from our transactional views of relationships. In order to do that, we will need to remove that scab and unveil the judgments we harbor. Then we can protect our wounds with an understanding of God's love, and connect with community.

❧ *Recalling Your History Exercise*

Write or tell a story about finances from when you were growing up. How did your family handle money? What did they think about it? Did your parents fight about money? Did they try to hide the fact that they were rich? Did they conspicuously consume, even though they were poor? What did they do when or if they ran out of money?

❧ *Exploring Your Attitudes About Money Exercise*

Finish the following sentences, as quickly as you can.

I think rich people are . . .

I think poor people are . . .

God blesses us with . . .

When I'm doing well financially, I feel . . .

When I'm struggling financially, I feel . . .

God thinks rich people are . . .

God thinks poor people are . . .

When I want to show my love, I . . .

If I made a lot of money, my parents would feel . . .

When it comes to money, God wants me to be . . .

If I had money issues, I would rely on . . .

Now look at your answers. Can you identify if money has been a spiritual influence in your life? Has it had a healthy influence? Are you engaged in transactional relationships in your life? How does money affect your relationship with God?

❧ *Facing the Numbers Exercise*

Often we don't want to think about our exact financial situation, in our marriages or even with ourselves. But when we hide our debt, our guilt and shame can compound. In this exercise, we will look at the debts and how we spend money, then we'll recall God's love in the midst of it.

Add up your debts and assets. How do the numbers make you feel? Now as you look at those numbers, remind yourself that your worth is not dependent on whether you are in the black or the red. God loves you, no matter what your bank account says.

Track your purchases on one list for a week. Write down every coffee you buy and every phone app you purchase. Don't forget all the service fees and late penalties. Look over the purchases. What did you spend the most money on? Does your list reflect your spiritual priorities?

Again, if you're looking at your list and feeling guilt and shame, forgive yourself.

✿ *Washing the Feet Exercise*

Read John 13:1–17, the passage where Jesus washes the feet of his disciples. Why does Peter say, "You will never wash my feet"? What does this story tell us about community? What does it tell us about being in need?

If you are studying this with a group, then wash each other's feet.

Chapter 9

BEING BORN AGAIN

It was right at 5:00 P.M. when I punched the clock.
I had been working at Crabtree & Evelyn, a soap
store at the Merchandise Mart. When it closed, I
assimilated into the massive stream of pedestrian
traffic on Wells Street in Chicago, trudging like cattle
in a herd. That morning, the weather felt so balmy
that I couldn't bear to put on my usual black suit.
Instead, I wore a white silk shirt and gray pencil skirt
and toted a bag in each hand.

When the bleating taxi horns and exhaust fumes
surrounded me, my thoughts gravitated to a heavier
weight on my shoulders. I hardly noticed when a tall
young stranger stepped out of the throng of people
walking in the opposite direction and stood in front
of me. When I looked up, I halted and gave him a
courteous "How can I help you?" smile. I was pretty
sure he wanted to know the time. As I tried to figure
out how I was going to access the hour for my new

acquaintance, he reached for my chest. His attention was as singular and focused as any gynecologist, as he spread his hand over my left breast. In an instant, he had a chance to grope every bit of it. I looked up and saw his smirking face, concentrating on this object that happened to be an intimate part of my body. Then, just as abruptly, he walked away.

It took a few seconds for the incident to register. It wasn't an accidental brush that might happen on an elevator to the embarrassment of both people involved, or even the creepy frottage that one might encounter from a heavy-breathing man on a crammed subway. It was a deliberate, intentional fondling, a clear violation that was made even more infuriating by my slow reaction time. *Why didn't I drop my bags and punch him or at least slap him? Why did I just stand there?*

I turned around and he started running. He was way too fast. I could never catch up with him. In a split second, a lifetime of anger erupted in me and I did the only thing that a self-respecting Mace-less woman could do in defense. I threw down my bags, raised my middle finger high in the air, and screamed as loud as I could, a string of words, the highlight of which was a four-letter syllable that began with "F." I used the word as a command, as an adjective, as the subject of my command, and the command again. I rounded it out by employing the word as an interjection, and kept releasing my uncreative tirade until he was quite out of earshot.

As my red-faced fury wore off, I crouched down and picked up my stuff.

Heaving my assembled bags onto my shoulder, I stood up and headed north again, muttering at myself about what I should have done to the man, until my eyes confronted a much taller adversary; namely, the massive brick building, with letters bolted into the side that read MOODY BIBLE INSTITUTE. And I said the f-word again. Miserably, this time, as if I'd hit my thumb while nailing my own coffin.

If someone noticed me from one of those windows at Moody, they would have seen me with my offending finger in the air, yelling, and maybe even jumping. That would never be acceptable behavior for a Moody woman, even if she were being molested in broad daylight.

That made me pause.

What exactly would have been an appropriate response in my situation? A smile and a "God bless you anyway, Brother"? Should I have reached for that "sword of salvation" and quoted Bible passages to him? I'm pretty sure reciting Ephesians would've taken too long, and I wasn't convinced that the perpetrator would have gotten the point of my fury as I stumbled over the King James vernacular. Or was I expected to just keep walking, pretending that nothing happened?

Breathing deeply, I looked down at my blouse and a sudden guilt mingled with my outrage. I was wearing a white silk shirt—with a lace bra. I could trace the outline of the delicate thread with my eyes. The blouse was baggy enough to be acceptable, but I should have accounted for the wind that exposed my flesh through the delicate material.

I remembered the millstone around my neck. I had caused that man to stumble. *It was my fault.* Of course he groped me. I shouldn't have presented such a temptation. My panic rose again with the added shame. I was going to be thrown out of school for sure.

Then another voice in my head began to speak. I had anger and shame, but something else created a trinity of emotions: injustice. I had just been sexually assaulted. Why would I automatically assume that I was to blame?

As I walked toward the building, worried that I would be kicked out, I realized in that moment that my religious education at Moody wasn't preparing me for a lot of the issues I faced day to day. Moreover, it had planted a worldview in my head that was harming me.

I was more afraid of my system of beliefs than I was of a sexual predator. I felt guilt because the outline of my breast was exposed under my clothes. I felt shame because of my body—my own flesh and blood.

I looked down at my lacy bra and a flood of Moody

women flashed in my mind: the pastor's daughter who discovered that her brother had drilled holes into her bedroom wall so he and his friends could watch her changing; the woman who ended a date being felt up by a man who forgot to mention he was married; another woman who was raped, got pregnant, and kept the baby. In every instance, the women blamed themselves. They'd been taught to.

I heard stories regularly, pouring out of my friends as if I were a priest in a confession booth. I also heard the assessments. She should have done something more to cover herself. She shouldn't have had a drink that night. We all knew that alcohol invited trouble. She should never have been alone with a man. She ought to have fought harder or longer. She should have, somehow, kept it from happening.

We blamed ourselves for the assaults, just as we were taught, as the guilt crushed us. The *fault* stayed with us, as it had from the beginning of the Bible itself. We all knew the story of our culpability. It stood from the genesis of time. When the man bit the fruit, he blamed the woman for his deeds as well as her own, and the world transformed from paradise to misery. It was the Eve effect: women were the tempters, destined to play out that role in the world's tragedies forever. Even when we became victims of sexual violence, our religious tradition heaped guilt on us, and injured us all over again.

As I made my way up to my dorm room, I ached with shameful exhaustion. My religion became too much for me to bear. I took off my skirt and bra and slipped into the sheets in my silk shirt.

I felt entangled in the dark side of patriarchy. It made a stranger feel as though he had access to intimate parts of my body. It made me think that the violation was my fault. The patriarchal thinking had been passed down in the myths of my religion and had been clear in the dispensations that I learned. But I could no longer embody this image of Eve. I could no longer look to men to save me, nor could I be responsible for their downfall. I was having a crisis of faith.

UNDERSTANDING PATRIARCHAL RELIGION

I talked with Sue Duffy about everything, including my faltering faith. Throughout the conversation, Sue repeatedly encouraged me, "Carol, it doesn't have to be that way. It just doesn't. There are other churches." So I found another church.

I went to LaSalle Street Church, which was known for providing services to people living in the projects. The church was strongly committed to social justice. They saw themselves as a buffer between the rich and the poor and always imagined ways they could impact the neighborhood. With my mounting frustration living in between the Gold Coast and Cabrini-Green, I could be a part of a body that worked to ease the inequities.

An up-and-coming writer named Philip Yancey taught a Sunday school class at LaSalle. He had written a book about being disappointed with God, and he was working on one about grace. All of it felt right, so I attended the next Sunday morning.

Rev. Annette Huizenga preached. Her sermon was about verses in the Bible that she wished were not there. I sat thinking, *You've got to be kidding me.* My first foray with the liberal side, and they want to throw out the Bible. I folded my arms, crossed my legs, and tilted my head to the side while she began to talk about the passages in the Bible where women were abused or when slaves were told to obey their masters. She didn't flinch. She didn't try to explain the abuse away with the cultural norms at the time. She looked directly at those terrifying texts.

My mind traveled through the Hebrew Bible. I had read every word several times. I knew all of the difficult stories, even when they had not been echoed in Sunday school. I never heard the narratives from the pulpit, but when I read the Bible questions kept haunting me: *What was she thinking about all of this? How did she view God's promise?* What was Hagar, Sarah's slave's perspective when Abraham had sex with her in order to fulfill God's promise? What about Hagar's cries to God when she was exiled out into the desert?[1] Why did God's voice to Abraham command abusive, near-death experiences for both of his sons?

I thought of the Levite's concubine. She didn't have a name, but her story remained in the book of Judges. She was raped and ravaged all night. Then the Levite cut her into twelve parts and sent her body parts to the twelve tribes of Israel.[2]

I imagined Esther, whose story comes off as a glamorous fairy tale in our Sunday school classes. I wondered if Mordecai received some sort of payment when Esther became part of the king's harem. Was she sold as a sex slave? She's afraid to go into her husband's room without an invitation. She's an abused wife. Why haven't I ever heard anyone talking about the domestic violence?

I thought of Gomer, Hosea's wife, who was bought as a sermon illustration. She was a sex worker when Hosea bought her, and she went back into her former work. Evidently, sex work was better than hearing about how your husband only desired someone so despicable because God commanded it.

The church has not done well with the legacies of women, automatically making them into eternal virgins (like Mary) or promiscuous (like the woman at the well). It felt that the whole of theology was tainted with a virgin-whore complex. In our interpretations, we distilled the fullness of women's lives to their acts as sexual beings.

O God, I sat back on the pew and prayed. *The pastor's right. There are many things I wish were not in the Bible.* She wasn't throwing out the Bible. By lifting up the texts, she actually took the Bible seriously. She wasn't trying to make the scriptures into a feel-good glossy message, giving us three points and a weekly boost of "go get 'em" from God. She examined passages we ignored, and presented contexts where no one else dared to tread.

The sermon ended, with the loose ends dangling and the questions unanswered. I left having gotten one of the most important lessons of my life—it was okay to wrestle with the text and ask the questions. Annette had introduced me to the "hermeneutics of suspicion," or interpreting the Bible with a critical eye, while modeling how to stay engaged. A vigorous student of the Bible *had* to ask difficult questions. It was okay to wish cruel and inhumane stories and commands were not in the pages. If you took the text seriously, then that's what you had to do. If you wanted to reclaim your spirituality, then that's what you had to do.

As I walked back from church to my dorm room, I wasn't sure if I wanted all the gruesome stories taken out of the Bible. There was something good about having the narratives in our holy text. I knew what it was like to have my own stories questioned and erased. I was supposed to hide them, keep them on the down low to protect my family and my faith. I needed to pretend they didn't happen. People often wanted to get rid of the abuse by getting rid of the stories, but they ended up erasing me along with the experience.

So there was something important about these stories of women being in the Bible, because no one had edited them out. Somehow the words did give voice to the horrors of women. I wished that the stories were not there, in the sense that I wish that the violence never happened. But violence did happen and had kept happening since those ancient times. And so the narratives ought to have a part in our history of liberation and salvation.

I thought of the dispensations I had been reminded of so often at Moody, the line on the chalkboard that divvied up the promises and covenants that God made with men. Wasn't a woman's witness to God's saving work just as important? I thought about them—Hagar; Esther; Gomer; Mary, Mother of Jesus; Mary Magdalene; and Tabitha. Many of them overcame great cruelty in order to find liberation and to be God's agents of salvation for their people. We didn't tell their stories much, and if we did, we glossed over the abuse.

It doesn't have to be that way, Sue's voice echoed in my mind as I began to fill in the familiar line with their names, imagining how God poured out grace upon them, as I constructed my own subversive dispensationalism. We had the promise that the impregnated slave, Hagar, would be the mother of a great nation. The assurance was given to her as a mom who couldn't bear to hear the cries of her child. Perhaps that was the covenant of those who have the strength and courage to raise a child alone, the promise of divine sustenance in the wild.

We can draw strength from the hope of Esther, trained through beauty treatments and ritual sex in a harem. Even though she had been a violated teenager and a threatened spouse, she overcame years of domestic cruelty and brutal racism to understand that she would become the savior of her people. Perhaps she should hold the dispensation of courage for the abused.

What about the magnificent promises made to Mary, the unwed mother, who watched her stomach swell with the threat that her flesh would be stoned? She knew that she would be the most blessed among all women, that through her womb the hungry would be fed and the poor would be lifted. As the mother of God, she could bring the promise of salvation to the world in a way that no mere man could. Surely she would represent the dispensation of grace that God gives to those who open themselves to rebirth.

I heard the voice of the Samaritan woman at the well, whose theological discourse with Jesus was longer than any other recorded in the scriptures. Every preacher I knew had maligned her reputation, speaking about the fact that she had six husbands with a judgmental tone that I never heard when they talked about Solomon and his three hundred wives. But Jesus entrusted her with the truth that he was the Messiah, and she turned around and told the city about him. She would represent those who bore the truth of God.

Or the other Mary, the one who lavished the ointment on Jesus before his death, preparing his body for the crucifixion. Jesus said that we were supposed to whisper her name each time we spoke the good news of the Gospel, even though one Gospel account failed to mention her name. Through Mary, God dispensed the grace of loyal friendship and love without abandon. Jesus told us to tell the good news in memory of her; surely she could fit on this line.

Then there was Tabitha, the disciple. She made purple cloth and pastored in the "church age." When she died, her congregation washed her cold flesh. Then God resurrected her. Her leadership in the church was so important she was raised from the dead. I could think of no better example of a pastor.

Each of these women embodied the saving work of God. Through the lens of Christianity, I learned at LaSalle, I reread these stories. I gained resilience through them—the strength of the single mom, the power of the abused, the creativity of the womb, the proclaimer of truth, the love of the friend, and the model of pastoral leadership. As survivors, politicians, mothers, and leaders, they spoke to me, showing me how I ought to live and witness God's grace.

How could we keep leaving out half the population when we talk about scripture in many of our churches? Eve was our only representative—not because of her partnership in God's saving work but because of her failure. The woman made it on the chart as the fallen temptress.

I read this differently. The stories of women opened as I constructed my subversive reading of scripture, paying attention to the silenced women.

AWAKENING

Since my awakening to the damaging effects of a patriarchal structure of religion and its institutions, I have worked with a steady stream of women who have been abused, assaulted, and raped, and many of them have that same stew of anger, guilt, and injustice. Often, I have witnessed them work through the pain of coming to terms with their religious teachings in the midst of it.

In church and other institutions, they were taught

that they were not "pure" because of the violation. Other times they were told that they were responsible. Still other times, they could no longer trust God, because they could not get past their image of the divine patriarch, sitting on his kingly throne with all his maleness on display. Or they imagined that God should have protected them, and so they worried that God had failed them. In each case, we've had to untangle patriarchy from religious belief. It's not easy, or even possible sometimes. We don't always realize that we're working under patriarchal conditions because we're so used to them; it's like not knowing when we're breathing polluted air.

Patriarchy doesn't refer to men. Instead, it is a system that promotes male privilege, or an unearned advantage that's available to men while it's denied to women. A patriarchal society is

- male dominated (positions of authority are reserved for men, and women leaders stand out because they're so unusual),

- male identified (ideas of what's normal or preferred are associated with men), and

- male centered (our focus remains on men and boys and what they do).

A patriarchal society has an obsession with control because patriarchy maintains its privilege through restraining women or men who might threaten it.[3] Women often bend to control in order to gain protection and provisions. Patriarchy is problematic because it values women in terms of their ability to satisfy men's needs and desires. This system of domination and control objectifies and exploits women, and it can lead to violence against women.

In the religious arena, Christianity remains male dominated, identified, and centered through our masculine ideas of God, by not allowing women to be in authority, and by building its theological systems based solely on the actions of men.

There is a model for patriarchy in certain understandings of salvation. Jesus submitted to the Father (even to death) and in that act, the Father provided for our salvation. Salvation for conservative Christians is one wherein a person asks Jesus into his or her heart, he or she submits to the will of God, and in return God protects and provides for that individual. It is a personal relationship, one that happens with a covenant between God and one person.

In the Bible, there is a recipe for patriarchy for the church that extends to the family. Just as Christ is the head of the church, the father is to be the head of the house. The mother and children lose autonomy because they are to submit.

Of course, Christianity didn't invent patriarchy.

It has underpinned many cultures. In ancient times, upper-body strength was needed in order to survive; brawn was important for hunting and agriculture. But our economy shifted its focus from agriculture to industry to technology and engineering. We rarely hunt a beast for dinner in order to survive; instead our upper bodies are hunched over a keyboard and a glowing screen. We no longer need those biceps in the same way, except to open the occasional jar of tomato sauce. Instead, we need intelligence to survive. So male positioning in society has changed, as women have moved into the workforce and the roles that define gender become more fluid.

The religious Right resists these changes in gender roles and identity. In the political sphere, conservative Christians believe in working hard to protect their ideal family and the notion thereof because a patriarchal society is foundational to their faith. They see a myriad of threats to this ideal: women having medical access they need (particularly in the area of reproductive freedom), women receiving equal pay for equal work, same-gender marriages, and a spectrum of gender identities. So conservative evangelicals work to push for abstinence education in schools, uphold heteronormative marriages, uplift the Quiverfull movement, and maintain biological-sex-identified restrooms.

We hear patriarchy in the public sphere when

outlier politicians and pundits scoff at the idea of
rape within a marriage (if two people are married,
the twisted logic goes, the wife is no longer in
control of her body). As the patriarchal ideal family
breaks down in society, the religious Right feels the
very foundations of their faith shaking. Faith and
patriarchy are so bound together that a company
having control over women's health care and
discriminating against same-gender couples are
considered "religious freedoms."

Many people outside of conservative churches
become bewildered by the discriminatory passions
of the religious Right. They don't understand, for
instance, why women getting less pay would be
considered a matter of faith, especially since better
pay would help alleviate childhood poverty. But, for
the conservative Christian, it makes perfect sense.
If women work outside of the home, making equal
pay, they upset the sangfroid of the family and thus
dismantle patriarchal Christianity. Understanding the
religious Right with the lens of patriarchy clears up
many mysteries.

For example, why is condom use acceptable, but
birth control pills are not? If they consider abortion
immoral, why would the religious Right work against
access to Planned Parenthood, which provides birth
control to women? It is because men have control over
condoms, but women take the pill.

If religious Right Christians uphold the sanctity
of human life, and uphold the Ten Commandments,
which clearly state we should not kill, then why is gun
control and military defense spending so important in
their political views? It's so that the father can protect
his family.

In cases of assault, rape, or domestic violence, the
actors in patriarchal thinking will have a difficult
time accusing a man because he is supposed to be an
agent of protection. So they will gravitate to blaming
the woman, even when it goes against logic. They do
this in different ways. They might say that a woman
is crazy or that she is overreacting. They might say
that she clearly misunderstood. Or they will lecture a
woman, "Don't wear a tight shirt," instead of telling
men, "Don't rape women."

MOVING FROM PATRIARCHY
TO PREGNANCY

Patriarchal Christianity can be very difficult to let go.
For many people, this covenant breaks down when
they do not feel completely protected. When illness,
sickness, or death occurs, people blame God. The
Christian feels that illness is unfair or that death is the
ultimate betrayal.

Why would this be? We are all mortal and we will

all die. Why would people blame God for the death of
someone who naturally passed away in her old age?
Of course, the pain and confusion of grief cause us to
ask, "Why, God?" And it is a natural, holy response.
Yet, for some people, a person dying goes against
their idea of God as our protector and reflects the
breakdown of our patriarchal understanding of God.

How can we begin to dismantle this idea? There
are many life-giving ways to understand God within
Christian tradition. One ancient idea is called
"panentheism" (not to be confused with pantheism).
Within this tradition, we can let go of thinking of God
as a Father to please and instead as more of a Spirit
who works in and among us. We can imagine that
God is pregnant with us, that God is pregnant with
the world. It is in God that "we live and move and
have our being."[4]

When a loving mother suffers a miscarriage, it
would be cruel to fault a mother for the loss. Instead,
we honor her grief and suffer with her. In the same
way, when we suffer wounds, we can understand the
nurture and comfort of God, who is the source of all
life. Through this shift, we move from understanding
salvation as an individual act of submitting to the
Father to realizing that we work alongside God for the
salvation of all creation.

This way of thinking outside a patriarchal model
of religion made me aware of the beautiful idea that

God saves us not in a solitary act of a murmured prayer but through pulsing, vibrant community. It is not because of our individual striving or saying some magic words. The act of salvation begins and ends with God, and we can participate in it if we wish, for God is pregnant with us and all of creation.

BORN AGAIN AGAIN

The first time I rejected the model of Christianity I learned throughout my whole life was during the summer before I graduated from Moody. I was home in the Florida humidity that coaxed the corners of the grass-cloth paper to curl off the walls. Seeing the paper reminded me of the sacrifices that my parents made. They went without air-conditioning in the Florida heat to pay for my Bible school.

I was thankful for my parents and for the many people who contributed to my education, but I had come to the realization that I could no longer drink from the same theological stream that they did. It was too poisonous for me. So I tried to appreciate the education for what it was: an opportunity that allowed me to grow spiritually. It offered me the chance to flourish in my own understanding of God.

I felt so out of place in the familiar living room. It shrank somehow, and my family had become different people. Of course, that wasn't the case. The walls didn't diminish. I had grown. My parents hadn't morphed. I had.

During that trip home, I fell asleep in the back of my mom's car. My mom was driving and my sister was in the passenger's seat. I had a transformational dream. I was sitting on a pew, looking at a table. I realized I was replaying a scene from the Hebrew Bible. I was Hannah facing Eli the priest, who thought I was drunk.[5]

Eli watched me with his scorn. I wasn't inebriated, but his glare incited shame nonetheless. I knew that I needed to make the sacrifice on the table for my guilt, but I didn't have any grain. Suddenly stunned, I realized Hannah had been willing to give up a child. I cried to Eli, "I can't! I don't have a child. I couldn't give one up if I did." My cries bounced off the hard temple walls. Eli seethed with the impatience of a sober man negotiating with a drunk. He kept looking at the table.

Then I understood. *I* was to be the sacrifice. I needed to crawl to the altar. When I got down on my knees, I saw broken glass covering the floors. I called out in agony. I started to wake up with my knees crammed and aching. Half-asleep, I blurted out, "I can't do it anymore. *I can't!*"

My mother responded, "What?"

"This whole thing," I said, "You know they're

watching me? All the time. At school, someone is always there, waiting for me to screw up. Their whole goal in life is to make sure that I behave the way that they dictate, so that I'll think the way that they think and act the way that they act. Women aren't allowed to have their own lives or careers. I can't take it anymore. I'm sacrificing too much of myself."

"Honey, I don't know what you're talking about," my mom started.

My sister interrupted and assured me, "It's okay, Carol. A lot of people change career paths in college. Plenty of people in our occupational therapy school graduated and decided the job wasn't for them."

Relief washed over me. Leah understood. "It's more than just the program though," I confessed. "It's the whole thing." It was wrong for me to keep going forward on that glass, the shards of my broken self, shattered on the ground, but I couldn't leave the altar room either. I looked at my mom. My heart swelled and I knew that I was afraid of losing my family.

When I began to chip away at the fundamentals of my faith, or even when I asked too many questions, not only did I fret losing my eternal salvation, but I also worried my friends and family would turn their backs on me. If I left Evangelicalism for a more liberal movement, it would be a worse offense than parting with Christianity altogether, because then I would be on the other side of the aisle. I would become an enemy.

Conservative Evangelicalism takes hold in our homes, like a dog that refuses to let go of a chew toy. If you try to shake it, you end up getting bit, especially because socialization comes with cutting off and shunning of those who question.

My dream depicted my fear: If I remained in my faith, I would continue to wound myself. But I was afraid that my family would cut me off if I chose another spiritual path. I had to either sacrifice myself or sacrifice my family. I wanted my family. I burned with anger and resentment. *Why did Evangelicalism force me to choose?*

When we reached home, I was still haunted by my dream and the implications. I retreated to the beach. I ran into the waves, kicking and beating wildly and swimming as fast and as far as I could. When the turbulent ripples turned glossy and smooth, I turned onto my back and began to float on the briny surface. I breathed deeply, and the ocean surrounded and lifted me. What was left of the anger, resentment, and fear dissipated into the sea the way hard grainy bath salt becomes oily and soothing. The seagulls circled above, and even though my ears were under the water, I could hear their curious squawks. My chest rose and fell in regular rhythm in the stillness.

Then arms grew up around me, encircling me. There, in the enormity of the ocean and sky, they embraced me. I began to remember the words

of Jesus, "You must be born from above."[6] I had
described myself as "born again" thousands of times.
I became born again at the Sunday evening service
at our Baptist church as we sang our tenth round of
"Just as I Am." I became born again at Bible camp. I
became born again at Christian concerts. But I never
realized that if I were to be born of God, then God
had to be a mother.

Yet, at that moment, God surrounded me and I
sensed her, delighting at the smell on the top of my
head. She was a fierce mom. A good mom. She was a
mother who would love her children, no matter what
that child might do and no matter what her child
might believe. God would mourn with loss and rejoice
with pleasure.

The arms felt so real that, somehow, I realized I no
longer had to live in constant fear of losing God's love,
or anyone else's love. God didn't withhold favor based
on a particular belief system I might be testing at the
moment. God was not over me, judging me, waiting
for my missteps. God was under me, grounding me.
My faith didn't have to be a constant struggle to
win God's approval and to demonstrate that I was
still good, because God was *for* me. In my faith, in
my wrestling, and in my doubt, a community and a
tradition of thought buoyed me.

As my body bobbed on the surface of the water, it
didn't matter what I believed or just how I believed

it, because beyond crashing waves of anger, dizziness, sorrow, doubts, and questions, in the vast enormity of that ocean, God got a lot bigger.

❧ *Finding Wholeness Exercise*

CREATE YOUR RECLAMATION SPACE. At the beginning of this process, we were intentional about carving out a space of time and location. Now, we will want to find peace in this process by filling that space with a small altar, as a reminder of how you have been "altered."

You have spent time locating your wounds, removing that overprotective scab, and allowing your soul to be vulnerable once more. Now, you can sort through the wisdom you have discovered in this process and nurture your connection with God.

REFLECT ON YOUR COLLAGE AGAIN. Now that you have spent some time reading, studying, and reclaiming parts of yourself, pull out your collage. Do you see anything there that you didn't notice before? Would your picture of wholeness look different now? Do you need to create another collage? Do you want to pull out one image or cut out unhelpful pictures? Add your collage, or a part of your collage to the space.

RECLAIM WHO YOU USED TO BE. Is there

an object that reminds you of the faith of your youth? For me, it's my old Bible, which I read through many times. It has marginal notes that make me cringe, but I hold it because my background gave me the gift of knowing the words.

WRITE DOWN YOUR METAPHOR FOR GOD. We all have different metaphors, but what is yours right now? Has it changed? Can you add an icon, picture, or object that reminds you that God is love?

WHAT HAS BEEN IMPORTANT FOR LEARNING TO LOVE YOURSELF? Was there an object, a drawing, or a ritual that you would like to include in your space? For instance, I would include a wonderful ornament of Frida Kahlo that my friend Jes Kast gave me, a rock from Rhode Island, and anointing oil from Thistle Farms.

WHAT IS THE DREAM OF GOD? When you think about the world as it ought to be, what does that look like? Can you draw, write, or sing what you imagine when you pray "on earth as it is in heaven"? Place that in your space.

It was another one of our Saturday morning outings to
the north part of Chicago. The cool wind was blowing
as Brian took me to a cemetery and we examined
historic grave sites—the worn granite, the marble
mausoleums, and the angelic sculptures. Our friendship
had deepened, until we started dating, and it was just
like Brian to take me out to a graveyard. Then we got
to a statue of death, grimly looking down at us.

At the site of him, Brian stopped me, pulled out a
ring, got on one knee, and recited the Song of Songs:

> *Place me like a seal over your heart,*
> *Like a seal on your arm;*
> *For love is as strong as death,*
> *Its jealousy unyielding as the grave.*
> *It burns like a blazing fire, like a mighty flame.*[1]

We were married in Florida, along the warm
breeze of the river. We continued our education in

seminary and moved to South Louisiana. We had a
daughter and named her Calla, after Diego Rivera
and Frida Kahlo's paintings of calla lilies.

As I was writing this manuscript, I got an e-mail
from a New Testament professor. She had been
reading some of my work in the *Christian Century* and
wanted to know if I would teach a Doctor of Ministry
course with her at the University of Dubuque
Theological Seminary. I was thrilled at the prospect,
and as we continued our introductions, I was
stunned to find out that she was the Rev. Dr. Annette
Huizenga, who was once the pastor of LaSalle Street
Church. She had no idea that I had ever attended
LaSalle or that she had such a huge impact on my life.

My father died after many years of continued
strokes. He did not go gently into the night. He fought
the passing, like Quixote fighting the windmills.
Eventually he gave in and let death wash over him.
I visited him the day before he died. It was Mother's
Day and I silently prayed that God our Mother would
surround him.

That day, my mom and I were not enjoying some
decadent chocolate dessert, our custom on any other
Mother's Day. And I was far away from my own
daughter, feeling the weight of empty arms. Instead I
was by my father's hospice bed, the contraption that
had made a way for home nurses, oxygen tanks, and
comforting opiates.

The morning light splattered through the east window, leaving golden speckles across his sheets. I breathed in the smell of the bleach that held the mold at bay, and I noticed a tinge of decay. It was that particular smell that came with sallow skin and a tilt of the head, signaling the end. I wanted to be with my mom if my father died. It seemed the least I could do on Mother's Day.

I sat, knowing that I had been there many times before, at that citadel of death. The end had been coming for a decade, but my father always mustered his tenacity and kept breathing. I looked down at his resting eyes, wondering if this would be another false alarm.

Seeing his serene face, I was sure I had forgiven him. "The beauty of death," my aunt told me, "is that forgiveness is final." I held his hand, looking forward to that finality.

He woke up. "Where's your mother?" he asked, his voice graveled with irritation. I wondered if that was it—if I had traveled there for this peevish blurt, my dad wishing I were someone else. This was our moment for strained amends, affirmed love, and whispered promises. I had read about it, seen it in movies: the gift of prolonged dying, when everyone holds their breath in anticipation. But I just got this grumpy question.

"She's in the living room, watching TV," I

answered, wishing that the morphine drip had made
him more pleasant. Then I dutifully fetched my mom
and walked outside.

I shouldn't have been annoyed that he didn't
want me. It was probably a bedpan emergency,
and he didn't want the indignity of his daughter
handling it. But I had made the trip. I had stood
up a congregation where I was to be the guest
preacher. My savings were dwindling with each
flight. I was hoping he would be a little bit pleased
to see me.

I didn't want our exchange at his bedside to be our
last. And I did say many more words. I prayed over
my dad, asking God to lead him to green pastures
and beside still waters. I reminded him that nothing
would separate him from God's love, and I was
comforted by the thought that death might finally
close the lonely abyss that haunted his mind. But he
died when I left, without speaking to me again, and it
didn't seem fair.

We had the funeral. Our eyes were dry, and our
loved ones said things like "It's probably better"
while we nodded. The process of dying was long,
and he was difficult, and we all knew it. The pastor
understood our family well enough to paint a realistic
picture, not one of a glowing patriarch. We were
grateful. We have made our own ways to God on

different paths, but none of us has taken a sentimental road. The truth was what we wanted.

Dad was in the grave. He had makeup and a shiny box with satin pillows. Absurdly, the freshly torn earth was covered by AstroTurf. I was relieved that my father's suffering had ended and my mom could have her life back.

She did get her life back. Life went on for me too. I went to work pastoring, traveling, and pounding out words. Everything seemed normal—except that I lost weight and grew disoriented. Sleeping became something I no longer did on purpose. It overtook and captured me at odd hours; then it left me, abandoned. I lived in a fog of irritability and forgetfulness. Tears flowed at awkward times, unbidden and unwanted. Friends prayed for me, and for the first time, prayer felt like palpable sustenance. I was getting through the days by consuming others' hopes and yearnings for me.

Later I realized I had not forgiven my father. It was when I read the passage of Lazarus and heard Jesus thundering, "Unbind him, and let him go."[2] The words echoed through me. My resentments had bound me to my father, even in his death. I had been afraid that without them, there would be nothing left of our relationship—nothing there to bind us. So I had secretly nursed discontent and an unwillingness to forgive. But then I heard that command of Jesus, booming through generations until it called up death itself: "Unbind him."

So I unfurled the linen pieces and peeled off the bandages. I gave the wounds air to breathe. I unbound him from my bitterness and acridity. As I let each piece go, I learned that love remains.

Acknowledgments ❧

As I hold this book, the words contain the echoes of
a multitude, people I loved and cherished along the
process, who chipped away at sentences, added sage
advice, and smoothed rough edges.

My mother, who has been an amazing support,
gave me the greatest gift—she told me that she would
not read the book. Since my mom is a writer herself,
I suppose she understood the freedom that I needed
with that promise. She was giving me permission
to write without having to worry about her looking
over my shoulder. It was a great joy to be able to
know I had her love and approval, no matter what
my spiritual convictions might have been in all of it.
She may never read these acknowledgments, but my
gratitude is overwhelming.

I am thankful for my brother and sister, Mark
Howard and Leah Showalter, who have worked
through many of the same wounds in different ways.
They have always been ahead of me on this path, and
I could have no greater guides.

I am grateful for Meredith Kemp-Pappan, Anna
Woofenden, Hollie Woodruff, and Megan Hansen,

who not only managed my travel and life, but encouraged me at every turn.

Many people read the manuscript in various stages and forms, giving helpful advice. They are talented writers, careful editors, and good friends. I'm grateful for Christian Piatt, Doug Hagler, Jamie McLeod, Candasu Vernon Cubbage, Jesse Quam, Ruth Everhart, MaryAnn McKibben Dana, Elizabeth Hagan, Leslie Klingensmith, Susan Graceson, Paris Akins, and Aric Clark. I stole pithy comments from a lot of them and incorporated them into the book. I'm also grateful for Bec Cranford and Jenny Warner, whose stories informed and inspired me. And I'm grateful for Ryan Kemp-Pappan and Lia Scholl, who listened to my anxiety as I fretted over the process.

Thanks to Derrick Weston and Rob Dyer. We have been working on a podcast together for years. And our readings and conversations have infused this book. I'm always grateful for their wisdom and friendship.

Lewis Donelson, my New Testament professor in seminary, has never quit teaching me. He has been a good friend as I write, answering random questions about Greco-Roman society. Frances Taylor Gench helped me think about being born again. And thanks to Annette Huizenga, the New Testament scholar who was my pastor and became my friend. I have deep gratitude for Cynthia Rigby and William Stacy

Johnson, my theology professors, who had great patience with me in seminary, as I sorted out my Bible school beliefs.

I'm grateful for Kathryn Helmers, my agent, especially as she encouraged me and helped shape the initial vision. There have been many writers who have been generous in giving me professional advice along the way—Diana Butler Bass, Phyllis Tickle, Meredith Gould, Brian McLaren, and Edward J. Blum. While writing, I had the opportunity to talk with some of our finest living memoirists. I plied Nadia Bolz-Weber and Sara Miles with questions one morning, over coffee. They may not even remember the conversation, but I do. They were invaluable in the process.

When I called Lauren Winner for help, she offered to work with HarperOne to do the bulk of the manuscript's reshaping. It was a monumental task, but Lauren knew just the right questions to ask to lead me through the process like a sage. Michael Maudlin, my editor at HarperOne, first encouraged me to start this book. The fact that he believed I could do it and continually encouraged my voice helped me grow profoundly, not only as an artist but as a human. And I am indebted to Anna Paustenbach, whose careful attention uncovered the heart of the story. The whole team at HarperOne has been extraordinary—Mark Tauber, Noël Chrisman, Ann Edwards, and Juliann Barbato.

My husband, Brian Merritt, not only walked this path of healing with me, but understood my vocation as a writer and gave me the time and space I needed. Much of this exploration left me raw, but he stood beside me through all of it. And, of course, Calla: her first kicks gave me so much joy, but they cannot be compared to the joy I experience as I walk with her each day.

Chapter 1: A Tree Grows in My Bedroom

1. Lemony Snicket created this tree in *The End,* the last installment of *A Series of Unfortunate Events* (New York: HarperCollins, 2006). I read the series to my daughter, and we were delighted by them. Little did I know then, that a central metaphor in this comedic children's book would be one that I would cling to throughout my religious healing.
2. Matt. 22:37, 39.
3. The stunning idea that God is *for us* is found in Rom. 8:31. Karl Barth also comes back to this simple prepositional phrase throughout his *Church Dogmatics* (Louisville, KY: Westminster John Knox Press, 1994).
4. Acts 17:28.
5. *Book of Common Worship* (Louisville, KY: Westminster John Knox Press, 1993).

Chapter 2: Finding Shalom

1. Names and details have been changed throughout the book.
2. Hosea 6:1, edited for inclusiveness.
3. I talk about "my pastor" as an official designation, but the actual person changed throughout the years. As I got permission from my family to tell this story, it was important to them to clarify that I'm not talking about Jamie Buckingham. We attended Jamie's church for many years, and since he is a well-known figure in some Christian circles, they wanted to be sure that I didn't unintentionally accuse him.
4. Mark 2:27.

5. For Jesus's refusal to stone the woman, see John 7:53–8:11. For the Law to which the teachers refer, see Lev. 20:10. For Jesus's healing on the Sabbath, see Matt. 12:9–14, Mark 3:1–6, and Luke 6:6–11. Exod. 31:14 requires the death penalty for those who break the Sabbath. Healing was considered work.
6. Lev. 15:19–24.
7. Matt. 22:34–40.

Chapter 3: Healing Our Image of God

1. 1 John 4:7–8.
2. Most of my work in this chapter is based on Sallie McFague, *Metaphorical Theology: Models of God in Religious Language* (Minneapolis: Fortress Press, 1982).
3. Andrew Newberg and Mark Robert Waldman, *How God Changes Your Brain: Breakthrough Findings from a Leading Neuroscientist* (New York: Ballantine Books, 2010), 19–20, 131–33.
4. Taizé Community, "Bless the Lord," *Glory to God* (Louisville, KY: Presbyterian Publishing, 2013), 544.
5. Matt. 7:13–14.
6. Serene Jones, *Trauma and Grace: Theology in a Ruptured World* (Louisville, KY: Westminster John Knox Press, 2009).
7. 1 Cor. 13:11–13.

Chapter 4: Recovering Our Emotions

1. Matt. 19:4–6, KJV.
2. Karl Marx, *Critique of Hegel's "Philosophy of Right"* (Cambridge: Cambridge Univ. Press, 1970), 131.
3. Hilary Jacobs Hendel, "It's Not Always Depression," *New York Times*, March 10, 2015.
4. The two books that have inspired me to think of God in suffering have been James H. Cone's works, *God of the Oppressed* (Maryknoll, NY: Orbis Books, 1997) and *The Cross and the Lynching Tree* (Maryknoll, NY: Orbis Books, 2011).
5. Ps. 23:4, my paraphrase.
6. Calvin first called the Psalms the "anatomy of the soul" in

his commentaries. Then Serene Jones expands on the idea in *Trauma and Grace.*

7. See Judg. 4 and 5 for Jael's story and John 11:35 for Jesus's.
8. This exercise was adapted from Thich Nhat Hanh's *Peace Is Every Step: The Path of Mindfulness in Everyday Life* (New York: Bantam, 1991).
9. Much of this exercise I learned from the Rev. Dr. Gene Fowler, a pastoral theologian who uses the psalms to help people through grief. He explores these ideas in *The Ministry of Lament: Caring for the Bereaved* (St. Louis, MO: Chalice Press, 2010).

Chapter 5: Redeeming Our Broken Selves

1. Luke 15:11–32.
2. This number comes from a Media Dynamics, Inc., study from 2014, http://sjinsights.net/2014/09/29/new-research-sheds-light-on-daily-ad-exposures/.
3. Deut. 30:19 and Matt. 10:12–14.
4. James 3:5–10.
5. "Your Inner Voice: How to Talk to Yourself and Why It Matters," *Psychology Today*, June 2015, 50–59.
6. Gen. 35:7.
7. Matt. 16:18.
8. Ps. 62:2.
9. From Mark 1:11. This exercise was adapted from a discipline that I learned from author and minister, Chris Glaser.
10. I want to be careful and clear here. When I write "Can you forgive yourself?" I don't mean to imply that you need to forgive yourself for being gay or having sex.

Chapter 6: Reclaiming Our Bodies

1. St. Augustine, *Confessions* (London: Penguin Classics, 1961).
2. St. Augustine, *On the Trinity, Books 8–15*, ed. Gareth B. Matthews (Cambridge: Cambridge Univ. Press, 2002), 91–92. I'm relying heavily on Rosemary Radford Ruether's "Augustine: Sexuality, Gender, and Women" in *Feminist Interpretations of Augustine*, ed. Judith Chelius Stark (University Park: Pennsylvania State Univ. Press, 2007).

3. Gen. 1:27.
4. Gal. 3:28.
5. Russ Taff, "Medals," in *Medals,* Word, 1985.
6. Matt. 26:6–13, Mark 14:3–9, Luke 7:36–50, and John 12:1–8.
7. Adapted from the Eucharistic words of Jesus found in 1 Cor. 11:24 and the creation story found in Gen. 1:27.
8. Ps. 139:14.
9. I learned these exercises, as well as much of what is in this chapter from the directors of Sanctuary for the Arts, Amy Shoemaker and Jeffrey Cheifetz.
10. Portions adapted from the Church of England's liturgy at https://www.churchofengland.org/prayer-worship/worship/texts/pastoral/healing/layingonhandsathc.aspx.

Chapter 7: Regaining Our Hope

1. Abraham Maslow, *Motivation and Personality* (New York: Harper, 1954).
2. "Meister Eckhart: Sermon 2," in *Essential Writings of Christian Mysticism*, ed. Bernard McGinn (New York: Random House, 2006), 35.
3. *Book of Common Worship* (Louisville, KY: Westminster John Knox Press, 1993), 69.
4. Luke 1:46–55.
5. Luke 17:21.
6. Matt. 6:28.
7. The promise that we can never be separated from God's love is in Rom. 8:38–39.

Chapter 8: Reassessing Our Finances

1. Timothy E. W. Gloege, *Guaranteed Pure: The Moody Bible Institute, Business, and the Making of Modern Evangelicalism* (Chapel Hill: Univ. of North Carolina Press, 2015). My conversations with Timothy Gloege and studying his work helped me to understand and undergird the relationship between individuality, capitalism, and evangelicalism.

2. Edward J. Blum, *Reforging the White Republic: Race, Religion, and American Nationalism, 1865–1898* (Baton Rouge: Louisiana State Univ. Press, 2005). Location 3139. I'm indebted to Ed Blum's insights for much of this chapter.
3. Kate Bowler, *Blessed: A History of the American Prosperity Gospel* (Oxford: Oxford Univ. Press, 2013), 7–9.
4. Exod. 22:25; Luke 16:13, 6:30–36.
5. Friedrich Schleiermacher, *The Christian Faith* (New York: T&T Clark, 1999), *132*.

Chapter 9: Being Born Again

1. Gen. 16, 21.
2. Judg. 19.
3. Allan G. Johnson, *The Gender Knot: Unraveling Our Patriarchal Legacy* (Philadelphia: Temple Univ. Press, 2014).
4. Acts 17:28.
5. 1 Sam. 1.
6. John 3:7.

Epilogue

1. Song. 8:6, NIV.
2. John 11:32–44.

Further Reading

Edward J. Blum, *Reforging the White Republic: Race, Religion, and American Nationalism, 1865–1898* (Baton Rouge: Louisiana State Univ. Press, 2005).

Kate Bowler, *Blessed: A History of the American Prosperity Gospel* (Oxford: Oxford Univ. Press, 2013).

James H. Cone, *The Cross and the Lynching Tree* (Maryknoll, NY: Orbis Books, 2011).

———, *God of the Oppressed* (Maryknoll, NY: Orbis Books, 1997).

Meister Eckhart, "Meister Eckhart, Sermon 2," *Essential Writings of Christian Mysticism*, ed. Bernard McGinn (New York: Random House, 2006).

James F. Findlay Jr. and Dwight L. Moody, *American Evangelist, 1837–1899* (Chicago: Univ. of Chicago, 1969).

Timothy E. W. Gloege, *Guaranteed Pure: The Moody Bible Institute, Business, and the Making of Modern Evangelicalism* (Chapel Hill: Univ. of North Carolina Press, 2015).

Gustavo Gutiérrez, *A Theology of Liberation*, trans. Caridad Inda (Maryknoll, NY: Orbis Books, 1973).

Thekla Ellen Joiner, *Sin in the City: Chicago and Revivalism, 1880–1920* (Columbia: Univ. of Missouri Press, 2007).

Serene Jones, *Trauma and Grace: Theology in a Ruptured World* (Louisville, KY: Westminster John Knox Press, 2009).

George Lakoff and Mark Johnson, *Metaphors We Live By* (Chicago: Univ. of Chicago Press, 2003).

George Lakoff, *Whose Freedom?: The Battle Over America's Most Important Idea* (New York: Farrar, Straus and Giroux, 2006).

Sallie McFague, *Life Abundant: Rethinking Theology and Economy for a Planet in Peril* (Minneapolis: Fortress Press, 2000).

———, *Metaphorical Theology: Models of God in Religious Language* (Minneapolis: Fortress Press, 1982).

Andrew Newberg and Mark Robert Waldman, *How God Changes*

Your Brain: Breakthrough Findings from a Leading Neuroscientist (New York: Ballantine Books, 2010).

Judith Plaskow, *Sex, Sin, and Grace: Women's Experience and the Theologies of Reinhold Niebuhr and Paul Tillich* (Lanham, MD: Univ. Press of America, 1979).

Walter Rauschenbusch, *Christianity and the Social Crisis in the 21st Century: The Classic That Woke Up the Church*, ed. Paul Raushenbush (San Francisco: HarperOne, 2007).

Dorothee Soelle, *Suffering* (Minneapolis: Fortress Press, 1975).

Judith Chelius Stark, ed., *Feminist Interpretations of Saint Augustine* (University Park: Pennsylvania State Univ. Press, 2007).

Becca Stevens, *Snake Oil: The Art of Healing and Truth-Telling* (Nashville: Jericho Books, 1994).